About the Author

Nomahlubi Jakuja is a development economist who has worked on a variety of projects, including developing a financial inclusion strategy for a leading African bank in twelve markets and the SADC Secretariat, research on mitigation strategies in South Africa, managing the United Nations Sustainable Food Systems Programme and developing a low-cost strategy for antenatal and postnatal classes in South Africa while having worked as a financial intelligence analyst at HSBC. Nomahlubi is currently working as a consultant for the World Bank Group on private sector reforms. Nomahlubi's goal in life is to be a key role player in Africa's development.

A Divine Set Up

Nomahlubi Jakuja

A Divine Set Up

Olympia Publishers
London

www.olympiapublishers.com
OLYMPIA PAPERBACK EDITION

A CIP catalogue record for this title is
available from the British Library.

ISBN: 978-1-80439-292-8

This is a work of fiction.
Names, characters, places and incidents originate from the writer's
imagination. Any resemblance to actual persons, living or dead, is
purely coincidental.

First Published in 2023

Olympia Publishers
Tallis House
2 Tallis Street
London
EC4Y 0AB

Printed in Great Britain

Dedication

This book is dedicated to all those seeking encouragement.

I could have chosen to write this book at any point of my storm, but I opted to wait for the dissipating stage for a couple of reasons. Firstly, it is difficult to have a clear perspective of the situation while in the middle of it. I had to go through all the stages of grief to finally get to a point where my head was clear enough for me to see the beautiful hand of God in all the difficulty.

Secondly, the Holy Spirit was still doing work in my heart that I believe needed time to manifest. The book would have taken a complete turn had I written in the beginning or middle stages of the storm. I doubt if it would have been an accurate account of my encounter with God.

I may not have known much about what God was revealing to me in the initial stages, but I knew the time for me to share my story had not come. My perspective of the storm has evolved so much. I am grateful I opted to wait in sharing my story. Lastly, but honestly, there is no greater healer like time, pardon the cliché.

I have a saying I often quote to friends; "Time takes away nothing, but only reveals what the eyes refuse to see." Let me tell you something about time. Whatever you refuse to see, admit or acknowledge, you need but only give it time. Believe me, whether you like it or not, by will or by force it will come to the surface, and you will have no choice but to see it.

My storm began, I believe, the day I ignored my intuition and decided to force my hand in marrying a man I no doubt loved at the time, but absolutely had no business being married to. The beauty of our God is His ability to honestly work all things for our good. Even situations we blindly or knowingly walk into.

This book is deeply rooted in my faith and is a detailed encounter of my journey with God. However, we all face storms, trails, and tribulations that I believe my story will help you in navigating and understanding. Also, God is not limited to those who acknowledge Him and have chosen to walk with Him, but I believe and know He is accessible to all who seek Him. If you are not a Christian or believer, I urge you to not put this book down. At the very least, continue for your own intellectual curiosity and love for storytelling.

Introduction

I was born into a spiritually divided family. My father oscillated between no belief and ancestral worship. On the other hand, my mom was what I call a "divided Christian." While she prayed and went to church, she also believed and participated in some of my father's practices and strongly encouraged and continues to encourage them among her children. Well, those who would listen.

Why is this important?

Our parents have a very important role to play in shaping our spiritual foundation, explicitly or tacitly. Everyone I have encountered has a childhood story that played a crucial role in what they believe. Whether it's the parents that forced them to go to church, the parents that did not, or simply a rebellion from whatever their parents practiced.

Having parents not united in what they believed meant I was not particularly forced into any direction. I went to church because my mom went, and later I began to enjoy this time with her. My personality type is not one that does anything half-heartedly. So, if I went to church, you'd best believe I went all-in. I participated in all things church from plays to Sunday school. What I did not realise is the deep foundation I was building and developing for my faith.

I subsequently went to a Christian boarding school where we had to go to church every Sunday, come rain or not. We were also encouraged to participate in other church activities as well.

While I took part in most of these activities, I will admit I was not the model Christian anyone looked to for spiritual guidance at this stage in my life. For those who went to a Christian school, I think right now someone comes to your mind when you think of a model Christian leader in high school. I absolutely was not this person. But I knew them and would often go to them when I felt spiritually depleted. I did not know it at this time, or rather it was not a well-defined principle of mine, but throughout my life and especially during the rebellious teenage years, I always found refuge and solace in church. I now believe most, if not all, the battles we face in life are spiritual. And to truly conquer any battle, you need a strong sensitivity to your spirituality. I believe this is especially true for those who believe their life has a purpose and are living beyond themselves.

Like most things in life, sensitivity to the spirit takes time and needs to be watered, nurtured and developed. Like most things, experience becomes the greatest teacher, with time being the ultimate fertiliser.

It would be years from my childhood and high school days to some of my most vivid encounters with God.

My belief is that random events are not a statistical encounter. I do not believe there is anything that happens in our lives arbitrarily. While the reasons for everything may not be revealed, and the reasons for others may be revealed in the moment or later in time, there still is a reason for every single detail and occurrence in our lives. I believe God works through our decisions and sometimes the decision of others. This is a hard pill to swallow, but has proven very true in my life. I don't consider myself a 'perfectionist' or risk-lover. In fact, I have a certain level of comfort with the unknown. But the idea that part of my destiny lies in the decisions of individuals connected to me was hard for me to accept. Especially when it comes to decisions that cause discomfort in my life. God honestly had to reveal this in my life. Otherwise, I'd still be convinced that God works in me, through me, and for me. But when God works for me, I believe He does so in the decisions of others. While the decisions may not come from you, they are for your own good.

I may not, and I know I have not, always acted with integrity. Here, I define integrity as your actions being in accordance with your will, thoughts, and desires. This is something I have always been highly sensitive to, because deep in my heart has been the need to align my thoughts, actions, and desires. One of the things that trips me up every time is when these facets of my life do not align.

In university I found my actions, desires and thoughts highly misaligned in so many areas of my life. I will start with my academics. My favourite courses in university were philosophy and economics, and much to my surprise these are the courses I struggled with. In my alma mater they used to publish the results of our exams outside each department after examinations. Every time I completed a philosophy or economics course, I genuinely believed I passed. Talk about the eternal optimist. Only looking back do I realise why I was disappointed most of the time. In my mind I believed I could get a pass, and this belief translated into seeing a pass every time. However, I think this very belief may have been the very reason I sometimes failed these courses. Maybe I missed the important tricks because I believed I knew and already passed. Whatever the reason was, I will never forget the look of disappointment every time the results were not favourable. The outcome just did not match what was written in my heart. I eventually dropped philosophy and continued with economics.

Another area that tested my integrity immensely in university was my church life. I participated in all things social in university. However, no matter what I had been doing in the week or on Saturday, I would always find myself at church on Sunday. I won't lie; it was not always the Holy Spirit moving me to church. Sometimes it came in the form of a cute boy or sheer procrastination from studying. I would find myself at the altar almost every Sunday, praying for repentance and deliverance. One Sunday I remember seeing a classmate of mine whom I always encountered at the altar for prayers and at the bar for drinks.

I remember asking myself, "When will he quit drinking or coming to the altar for prayers?" I judged him severely. But in observing him and judging him I was actually putting a reflective mirror to my life. It's funny that the people we judge the most are the ones that remind us of something in our own lives. Something we either refuse to acknowledge is wrong, or have acknowledged is not working but struggle to give up. It hit me hard that Sunday that I was this guy. My spiritual life was misaligned too. I believe this was the last Sunday I went to church. I decided to take an official break until I could align my actions with my will and desire.

This happened in the first year of university. What I did not realise was that I left church, but God never left me and I believe I never left Him either. We would begin a very deep relationship, one filled with very high highs and very low lows.

I could have never imagined that my decision to leave church was exactly the journey I needed to encounter God. I thought going to church was the route to discovering God. Actually, I was taught this growing up too.

I walked out, and did not return for a good two years. I continued my life of debauchery. My drug of choice was alcohol. I honestly cannot say I enjoyed the alcohol much, but with my understanding of children brought up in trauma-filled homes, I now understand why I stuck with it for much longer than just the experimental phase. What I hated the most about alcohol was the person I became every time I was drunk.

Let's go back a little bit. Hi, my name is Nomahlubi Jakuja. I grew up in a village called Dimbaza, where I experienced physical and nonphysical forms of violence both within my household and in my community. At the community level I experienced nonphysical forms of violence. Violence in the form of lost dreams. Violence in the form of lack of service delivery, which continues to date. Violence in having no community role models to look up too. Success is hardest to manifest when you have never seen it modelled by anyone like you.

Within my household, my father was an undiagnosed alcoholic. I genuinely believe he suffered from undiagnosed mental health issues or a severe case of unmanifested life expectations, of which we bore the brunt. He physically and verbally abused my mother. While he never physically touched me, the fear was deeply entrenched. I remember an encounter with him on one of his drunken episodes where he threw a heavy object at me, which I dodged. I honestly believe this could have broken many parts of my fragile body had it not missed. An encounter I shared with my mother, who minimised it to its bare minimum and to date calls me evil when I talk about it. So, pardon me if I misplace this violent scene. It is something that I never forgot, regardless of the name we gave it at home.

When you go through experiences that are not validated as a child, it really destabilizes you as an adult and makes you question yourself in situations of a similar nature. I believe it separates you from your intuition. You constantly second-guess yourself and don't trust your intuition much. The lack of validation of my feelings and experiences at home as a child meant I would have a great deal of trouble in intimate relationships where similar experiences needing to be validated were not.

According to trauma analysts, children who have experienced trauma in some form are more likely to engage in destructive and addictive behaviours compared to those who have never experienced trauma. Kids who have not experienced trauma can engage in addictive behaviours, and it never manifests into addiction. For those of us with trauma, we are likely to develop a habit and stick with this destructive behaviour much longer than necessary.

I remember during the 2010 FIFA World Cup, a friend of mine and I booked ourselves flight tickets to go to Johannesburg to be in the heart of debauchery. Of course, we did not call it this. It was all in the name of having fun, living our best lives or whatever you call it. You see, I have learned there is a fine line between having fun and recklessness. I am afraid for most parts I tended towards recklessness in the guise of having fun. After a night out, I remember me and my friends sitting in one of our friend's apartment and recalling the events of the previous night. I remember the feeling of distaste I had after that night. I prayed to God silently that, if He has not forsaken me, to please make a way back into my life. Boy, oh boy, was He listening. But you see, God is a gentleman. He only comes by invitation. That morning I invited Him into my life again. The morning after heavy partying and drinking, He was always telling me that this was not something I could sustain. But I found my actions, will, and desire highly misaligned.

Even after this cry out to God, I went back to my acquired habits. I remember going to campus one day, and there was a "Know your HIV status" drive on campus. I found myself wanting to know my status, but I remember the paralyzing fear I had. I did not have my status checked at this point, lest I start crying in front of the whole campus. But my desire to always be in alignment led me back to the campus clinic to get tested. My status was negative. I thanked God momentarily and went back to my old habits.

I can safely admit I struggeld to be obedient to God for reasons unbeknown to me. I am one of those people He literally has to either send heavy lessons to, or allow to be undeniably crushed in order for me to learn. This was especially true in relationships. At the end of 2011, during my third year, I found out I was pregnant. I spent the whole of my summer holidays contemplating my life choices, and had to hit a hard reset. Being pregnant at this stage of my degree would have meant adding an additional year to my studies. See, I was a government-sponsored student, so adding an additional year would have been a financial difficulty too. As if all of this was not enough, my studies had taken a serious beating too. I literally had no marks on my transcript. I had come to the University of Cape Town as an A-student, and was about to graduate with no marks, potentially a baby and absolutely nothing to show for it. I felt like I had wasted the last three years of my university life. Being the only one in my family to have ever gone to a university and the first one in my community to pass matriculation with distinction, I felt like a huge failure. Not only personally, but I felt the huge weight of every single child coming from a similar background as mine who had ever been given any opportunity for a better life.

I went to an Anglican Church back home which was no longer operational, and I sat outside the church door and poured my heart out to God. I managed to tell only one other person in my life about the pregnancy, apart from the father, and that was my best friend at the time. I went every day for most of my holidays to this church, as I found such great solace in just being there.

I told my boyfriend at the time, who was also the father of the baby to be, that I was pregnant. His reaction was soul-crushing. He asked if he was the father of the baby. This forced me into deep introspection. I could not escape questioning myself. While I make no excuses for his behaviour, I could not avoid wondering why he felt he needed to ask me if he was the father.

I decided to not keep the child. Days after telling him, my best friend and I took a forty-five-minute taxi to the nearest Marie Stopes, where I had my abortion and discovered I had an STI too.

Kwaze Kwaningi Jesu, Jesus this was a lot.

I found myself longing for church and questioning my decision to leave. I decided to go back to church and was determined to make the best of the one year left in my degree.

There are dreams you will never realise or see manifested in your life as long as certain people are in your life. We have heard this said time and time again in many forms and variations. *"The company you keep is important," "You are a product of the five people closest to you."* I beg to argue that you are the product of even the one person you keep whom you allow very close to you.

The year was 2012, the final year of my undergraduate degree. The year I would encounter God fighting for me for the very first time as a conscious and discerning human being. I use the words conscious and discerning to make it clear that God is always fighting for you, whether you are aware of it or not. From when you were formed in the place of utter seclusion, He knew you and has been fighting for you. My biology teacher in high school, Mrs Taylor, used to say that there are a million things that can biologically go wrong at birth, and every baby born healthy should be celebrated. I absolutely believe this.

If you earnestly invite God into your life and allow him to steer your ship, He truly will do the impossible. In 2012, He began by disrupting my closest relationships. You see, I had

19

two friends who enabled my destructive behaviour just by all of us behaving the same way. See, the devil knows we are very smart, highly educated individuals and will never use 'wrong' or the 'wrong' people to influence your choices. He uses good people. When people are 'wrong' for you, you can clearly tell. No matter how idiotic you are, you will not willingly enter 'wrong' spaces. No, the devil operates in the blurry line between good and right. He will use good people, who perhaps do not value the same things you value, or believe in what you believe, or do not have the same calling in life as you to get you into places and spaces you have no business being in. These are the very first people God will remove from your life when He is calling you out of certain places.

These are good people, so God will not leave this big decision to you, because He knows you will never make it. He will cause these people to reject you, make them think they are leaving your life or cause them to simply just stop talking to you. This is when you need to strongly overcome the spirit of rejection. If you must, go to therapy to overcome it. You see, absolutely nothing that is for you will ever leave you. All you need to do is not fight it. Do not ever fight to have anyone in your life who wants to leave.

God removed my two closest friends. They planned behind my back to find an apartment without telling me or involving me in the process. I could not fight this one even if I wanted to, as my mother could not afford an apartment for me. My option was very clear: student residence only. So, I moved to senior year residence. One of my roommates was a firm believer. I highlight her because for me she was a daily reminder of the person I wanted to be. I thought it no coincidence that I was next door to her. Anytime you are trying to kick any habit, having positive reinforcements is always great.

But God, He never takes away without sending double what you seemingly lost. That year I became very close with someone that had been in my life, as we did the same course and shared a lot of interests together besides our love for Jesus. I will never forget the way she loved me and accepted me. In fact, I hope and pray the kind of Christian I am is one that leads by example and never ever has to preach. I hope that my life and how I lead it will be a testimony on its own.

I do not remember ever talking about my dreams and hopes with the two friends that rejected me. I tried with one, when I changed degrees in first year from Finance and Accounting to Politics, Philosophy and Economics, and her response never again inspired me to share anything with her. She looked at me sternly and said, "well now I don't know what you are here for, maybe to count cows."

My Christian friend introduced me to her other friends. Wow. It opened my eyes into how other children were doing this student life thing. They had done semesters abroad, interned for large banks and consulting firms in the country and participated in literally all the societies at UCT (University of Cape Town). If anyone ever felt like the underachiever in the pack it was certainly me. I must thank God for my mother here, who instilled in me from a very young age a strong self-image and a confidence that was unmatched.

This did not intimidate me, but deeply inspired me. I went back to my room and started looking for internships in my field and applied. Honestly, there weren't a lot. My lack of understanding of my degree did not help either. But every Thursday they had career drives on campus. I decided to spend one Thursday there with the nerds and not drink the cool juice with the cool kids. TFG(Foschini Group) was there recruiting interns for their winter program. I took the flyer and thought about it. See, one thing about me that manages to set me apart is my ability to think and see an opportunity in the most obscure of situations.

For those unfamiliar with UCT, it is the Harvard or Oxford of Africa. All the smart and very ambitious kids at the top of their classes like the ones who will take over industry end up here; that is, if they don't literally go to Harvard or Oxford. The fox in me knew not a lot of my fellow UCT kids would be interested in interning at TFG. No, they were all headed for Goldman Sachs, or at the very least Genesis Analytics.

I realised if TFG had put in the effort to come and recruit, then they must be eager for UCT kids, regardless of what bunch of the pack they would get. So, I unashamedly submitted my transcripts filled with ink stains. Well, to my surprise they accepted me for their winter internship programme. I didn't think my new friends would be impressed, but I told them anyway. Oh my God, they were so supportive. They even offered me shirts and other formal clothes to borrow. I did not take them, but I appreciated the gesture.

God will write your name in the hearts of your future romantic partner, business partner, or anyone else, he will use in writing your story. During my internship I had a rotation with HR, and the head of HR remembered my name from the applications. She told me that when she saw my application, it reminded her of her own personal journey completing university with no work experience, and how someone had taken a chance with her. She admitted my transcript was not the most impressive, but my motivation letter moved her heart.

When I got back from my internship, literally the highlight of my university career thus far, I was on a high and could not imagine anything else God could do for me. See how little our vision is in comparison to the plans God has for us. One of my new friends had found an opportunity to potentially attend the prestigious One Young World Summit that was to be held in Pittsburgh in the United States of America. When she told me about it, a gathering of future world leaders, it immediately ignited a spark in me. It was now about July of 2012 and the summit was due to take place in October of the same year.

In an effort to respect my new friendship I did not immediately act on my desire to attend One Young World until maybe a month later. I had started implementing these quiet afternoons on Sundays to be by myself and reflect on the previous week and the week ahead. I decided to go onto the One Young World online page. I saw I had long missed the application deadline.

I thought to myself, "Well, I lose absolutely nothing by applying. If it's meant for me, God will make it happen."

I wrote the committee an email and I never expected a response because I had missed the deadline. To my surprise, they actually responded. They told me I had missed the deadline, but they appreciated my application. If I could find a sponsor and get my visa within the time left, they would accept me as a delegate.

Earlier, I shared that I do not do things half-heartedly. Well, this was no different. I lived and breathed One Young World. In Barney Stinson's words from the show *How I met Your Mother*, "challenge accepted." I went back to my friend who had also been accepted for the summit, and I told her about what I thought was a brilliant opportunity for both of us. She never shared her deep feelings with me, because she saw how excited I was and how I honestly did not see the looming competition ahead of us. To be honest, I was not completely oblivious to this. But, I knew as long as we did not go for the same sponsorships and kept the lines of communications open, it would not be a problem.

Well, she warmed up to the idea, and shared her funding strategy to date. It involved her networks back at home, various government departments, and applying at UCT. The university had paid for one of the wealthiest kids on campus the previous year, but had refused her application. Ever the defender of justice, this did not sit well with me. After our conversation I went home and was deeply troubled at UCT's decision to not fund her. So, the very next morning I stormed to their offices and had a lengthy conversation with the guy in charge. In the middle of the conversation, he asked me one of those thought-provoking questions. The ones that make morality and justice very difficult concepts to defend in real life. He asked whom I was actually fighting for here: myself, or my friend whom they had declined.

This question forced me to stop right there in my tracks and look at the situation again. I imagined a situation where

UCT had agreed to fund me. How would this land with my friend? I knew we had to diversify our approach to funding. Time was moving like a full river after experiencing heavy rains. I went home and did what I do best. I thought and looked at this whole situation from many different angles. I realised this was not the approach to follow, asking people to help who are not the least bit moved, like the guy I met at the UCT offices. Instead, I could approach it from a business angle and create a value proposition.

So, I translated the three-minute elevator pitch into a folder, printed a number of them and carried them everywhere I went.

I thought, "If I was a business person in Cape Town, where would I be found?" I mapped out a list of all the possible places business people might be found in the city. The believer that I am, I did not leave out the philanthropists from my list, including church leaders. We were now down to a month before the summit starts. The committee sent an email asking how I was doing. Honestly, I had not moved an inch since we last spoke. I am not sure what my response was, but I am confident it was a faith-driven one.

By this time, I had abandoned most of my classes and was down to attending only the ones I deemed essential. On my stakeholder mapping list, which I did not know at the time, I started at the Cape Town International Convention Centre, which was hosting the mining indaba. I dressed the part and carried my pitch. I laugh every time I think about this. My tiny self, trying to pass as a business person. This is how I know the grace of God was covering me. They let me in without a pass. I do not remember meeting anyone specific there. I probably left a couple of folders and left.

I spent a bulk of my time at the coffee shops outside parliament, chatting to parliamentarians. I realised here the power of a story and a strong why. Honestly, I know some people listened to the story and why I was there, while others thought I was crazy. I was now down to two weeks and nothing seemed like it had moved. What I now know and understand is how faith works. God had seen the effort I had put into this and He was doing what only He can do. In my walk of faith, I know God waits for you to exhaust all your human means so that, when He shows up, you will not confuse Him with anyone else, despite the human vessel He uses.

I had decided to resume attendance to all my classes because if this did not work out, I was not about to fail my final year as well. However, my faith was unshaken. I won't lie. I doubted. It was dark and it seemed impossible, and the time factor was not inspiring hope either. At this stage word among my friends had spread. Word was that I was going to the summit. I am not entirely sure how this came to be, but God will never fail His people. He will prepare a table for you in front of your enemies, not for their sakes but for His. He never forsakes His own. One of my friends had gone to an event in Stellenbosch two weeks before the summit, and met a guy working at the US embassy in Cape Town. This was a top person who gave her his business card and told her should she ever have any trouble at the embassy, to call him or simply say his name.

My good friend Thembi came to my room to check-in on me. She knew how invested I was at this point in time. She left the business card with me and told me that if there was still time, God could still come through. I'm honestly not sure how I was feeling at this stage. I can tell you that I never lost hope. It was one of those destiny moments where I knew God just had to show up. So many little things had affirmed in my spirit that I was going to go. The business card from Thembi sealed it. On Monday, I went to class and attended all my lectures. During my last lecture, which was politics, I caught wind that Mr Trevor Manual, the former Minister of Finance, was giving a lecture that afternoon at PD Hahn lecture theatre. The lecture was at five p.m., and my last class was at three p.m. To those that know me well, dressing the part is very important to me. There is just something I believe that sends a strong message about how you dress. Not in a superficial way, but in manner of self-expression.

I obviously was not dressed the part to meet a minister and a potential investor who would pour thousands into my vision. If I was going to ask this of them, I needed them to see the future me they were investing in. I left in the middle of my lecture and took a Jammie campus shuttle (bus) back to my residence, Forest Hill. Now, Jammies to Forest Hill in the afternoon are a nightmare. They operate every twenty minutes or so.

But I went knowing I was stepping into my moment of destiny. I put on my favourite pink dress with, grey stockings and brown shoes I had been given at TFG during my internship. I got back onto the Jammie. The Jammie had been instructed by the minister's security detail not to stop at the stop closest to the lecture hall for security reasons. When the driver did not stop, I asked him why, and he told me. I obviously knew that this was exactly the route I needed to take. So, he dropped me at the second stop and I walked back to the first stop. As I approached, I saw the minister and his security detail walking towards the lecture hall. I ran up to him like a little child would to their father.

His security detail tried to stop me, but he said, "No, let her walk with us."

I walked and gave him my three-minute elevator pitch. He said, "I thought this had passed."

I told him, "No it's on Wednesday, next week." He said a lot which I forgot. My head was absolutely somewhere else. All I know he did not say yes. He took my portfolio and reminded me it was not a yes. He walked into the lecture hall and asked if I was coming in. I honestly thought my job was done, but if there were any lessons my mother instilled in me, they were manners and decorum. So, I agreed and sat right in front.

When the question-and-answer moment came, I felt compelled to ask something, but I was not listening the entire time. My head was in a foreign country I had never been too, imagining all sort of things. There was someone sitting next to me who had a question, but they were shy. So, I asked if I could ask on their behalf. They agreed and I asked.

The minister and his people exited first and I went back to my room. I did not think about whether he would reach out or not. As a matter of fact, I did not think he would. But for me, if it ended right, then I was okay. It had showed me how far you really could go with faith, and that was all I needed to keep moving with my life.

No, no, no. God is a God of completion. He was not going to leave it there. The same week Wednesday a week before the summit, I got a call from someone from ABSA bank. They told me I was selected as part of their delegates, and would be attending the conference with their team as one of their ambassadors. I was so happy and over the moon. Now I never applied for any sponsorship with ABSA. I did not question how this came about. I accepted it as is. The very next day I went to the US embassy and used the name on the business card my friend had given me. I do not believe I had all the required documents at this point in time. If I did, they were all preliminary. I used this man's name. My visa documents were accepted and I got my visa the very next day. Not just any visa, but a ten-year one. I remember collecting my visa and thinking, "This is not the last time I'll ever go to America."

It was only in sharing this with my brother, who put the pieces together for me, that I understood. It was not a random call from ABSA. The minister's wife was the CEO at ABSA and he must have given her my portfolio. I remember praying to one day meet the minister or his wife to thank them. But I knew that even if I never met them, one way to thank them would be to do the same for someone else, should the situation ever arise.

Oh, but God is a God of completion. A year later, I met the minister's wife at a banquet and I was seated next to her. She did not know me. I reintroduced myself and thanked her. Trying to impress her, I told her of what going to that conference did in cementing my belief in myself and what I can do. I had attended the banquet on my way to do an internship in Brussels with NATO, the largest intergovernmental military alliance in the world, which I shared with her. I told her I would have never dared to apply for it if it was not for her sending me to the One Young World Conference. She was so kind; I think she gave me a hug. It is highly possible it was all in my head, but to me it was a hug nonetheless.

A Seed is Sown

I have always had the deep sense that I am not here on Earth merely to exist, but to do something bigger than myself. This resulted in frustration with things, people, and places that were not deeply aligned with what was in my spirit. I did not always have a clear vision of what exactly this mission I was put on this Earth for was. But that is the beauty that comes in accepting Jesus Christ as your Saviour. You do not need to see what that vision is in order for you to walk confidently in it; you simply just need to invite him in your life and He will do the rest. In a world where we are taught to work hard and bootstrap ourselves out of our circumstances, simply inviting God into your life and yielding to His ways can be a difficult concept to understand, and even harder to implement. I won't lie to you; this has been an area I have wrestled with God over for a long time.

I will try to unpack this as best as I can, but I believe it probably warrants a book all on its own. Inviting Jesus into your life and yielding to Him is sometimes misunderstood as being passive. As a matter of fact, many 'lazy' Christians perpetuate this notion. Laziness is a spirit that exists and will find any excuse to divorce itself from its duties. It exists all around and Christians are not exempt from it.

Yielding to God's ways means you need to have a heart after God's heart. This means utterly loving God and knowing that whatever should ever become of you, you will be okay. Let me explain even further. In John 4, Jesus encounters the Samaritan woman at the well.

In verse 14, He says, *"But those who drink the water I give will never be thirsty again."* Yielding to God means that you understand that drinking His water is all you need. You accept that if all He ever gives you is His water, then you will be fine. I must elaborate here, as this is often an area used by the enemy to deceive us into thinking God simply wants us to live literally on water and not prosper. If you know God, you know this is absolutely a lie. For how can a loving God who created the seas and heavens merely be satisfied with giving you just water? Once you are satisfied with the concept of being okay if He only gave you water, it means your heart is in the right posture to receive all God wants you to have in the land of the living, not in heaven.

Yielding to God means that as you implement your plans, either in your career, relationships or anything in this life, you understand and invite only His will to take place. Now, this is not a revelation I have always had. After submitting my life again to God in 2012, it would take me exactly ten years to have this revelation and understanding in my life.

Let's go back a little bit. Let me invite you into this journey. I could never talk about the One Young World Conference and not mention a divine encounter I had there. The conference opening ceremony took place on a ferry. There were a thousand delegates on the ferry from all over the world. I remember stepping onto the ferry with my roommate from Tanzania. She was meant to be the flagbearer for her country, so she was on a hunt for the person meant to give her the flag. I had no idea the ceremony was going to be so grand. I knew there were other delegates from South Africa, but I had not met any of them. So, I started walking around on the ferry on a mission to find the South African flagbearer. Instead, I saw a very striking, tall and devilishly handsome gentleman. He had such a natural command on the room. The kind that truly gifted charismatic leaders have. It came so naturally to him that I doubt he even knew it. I was immediately drawn to him. I thought of walking up to him, but for the first time in my life I was scared of someone. I allowed fear and doubt to paralyse me and I went back to my roommate.

Just as I was about to tell her, she asked me who the handsome gentleman behind me was. I looked back and, of course, it was my mystery guy. He came up to us *(in my head me)* and he confidently introduced himself. I honestly do not remember the rest of the conversation or the night. For me, having him walk up to us *(again me)* was more than enough. I never expected to see him again. I even forgot his name. After the ferry, I went back to my hotel room with my roommate and we called it a night.

During breakfast the next day, I noticed the tables were empty. There were probably five of us who made it for breakfast. The conference morning session was equally devastatingly empty. See, one of my personality strengths is significance. According to the Gallup Strengths finder test people with significance take joy in activities and tasks where they can be seen. So empty rooms disturb me a great deal. About lunch time the room was full again. After lunch, on my way to the bus for an excursion event we had to attend, I bumped into the mystery guy again. He walked up to me and we started talking. Now let me speak to some ladies. There is nothing more attractive than masculine energy to me. The energy that will walk up to you and introduce itself and even walk with you to your bus. In our conversation, I asked him if he noticed how empty breakfast and the morning session were. He told me he couldn't have because he was not there either. Upon further questioning he told me "Everyone" was at the club the previous night. He asked why he did not see me there.

Firstly, I knew it was an over-exaggeration, because my roommate and I were sleeping comfortably in our room. So not everyone was in the club. But I could not get over the fact that he noticed I was not there. What he did not know was that I had recently recommitted my life to God, and going to clubs was the last thing on my mind. Before we parted, he said he would find me that evening and take me to the club. I did not question this. In fact, I thought he was joking, since I did not give him my room number. But I immediately had a conversation with God about this club situation that I had just left. I told Him that if this man managed to find me in this big hotel, then I would go with him. The funny thing about our walk with Jesus is that like any relationship, it progresses in stages. In the beginning, He will allow you to tell Him what to do and fulfil your requests. It is His way of showing you that He is real and He hears you. But as you grow in your faith, you soon learn it is better to not tell Him what to do, but instead to allow Him to do what He does best.

That evening after supper. I was on such a high from the excursion that I forgot about the date I had agreed to. I got to my room and put my pyjamas on. Shortly there was a knock on the door, and it was my mystery guy. My roommate called me and when I saw this devilishly striking man at the door, I nearly dropped dead. I told him to give me a few minutes and then I'd come out. I grabbed a shirt and put on my jeans. My outfit was not impressive at all. He on the other hand was well dressed in a suit. He looked like a runway model running for office. Like that sexy combination of power and looks. Not one to be lacking in confidence, I walked right next to him as if I had the best dress on. I don't quite remember everything we talked about, but I remember the walk taking forever. Somewhere along the way a thought came to my head: what if he kidnaps me? See, he was from the United States, and he was studying at the University of Pittsburgh. It dawned on me that I either had a very good sense of people or I was completely naïve. I shared my concerns with him. He laughed at the fact that my trust issues were hitting me at night in the middle of nowhere with absolutely no means of reaching out to anyone.

We got to the club, and I could see he was immediately in his element. We walked in and he disappeared for some time. I mingled and met some delegates from South Africa. I relaxed a bit. I knew even if my mystery guy did not come back, I'd be okay. He continued to surprise me in a good way. He came back with a drink. I was so grateful. See, in my excitement I left the hotel without my wallet, cell phone, or anything really. A very good friend of mine once said that some of the deepest connections we will ever have in life are often brief encounters with strangers. I never forgot my mystery guy, and there was a deep connection I felt with him. I did not pay it much attention for many reasons. Mostly because I knew the next evening after the club encounter, I would be on a flight back to South Africa. We followed each other on Facebook, but we never texted or anything. It would be exactly ten years after our powerful encounter that we would reach out to each other again.

In my professional and personal life, I meet so many people that I am not sure if all of them serve a purpose or not. But I do believe in divine encounters. Make no mistake; when it is a divine encounter, you will know. There is a peace you will have about the person and situation. I felt at home with my mystery guy and I allowed God to do the work. I never felt the need to make anything work or manipulate anything with him. If I never saw him again, if he never came to my room, I would have been okay with it. A lesson I ignored exactly a year later.

I got back to South Africa a week later and completed my undergraduate degree at UCT. I graduated with an average of sixty percent, which meant I did not qualify for honours. I had not made any alternative plans, except to go to Rhodes University. They also declined my application. They said I needed a minimum of sixty-two per cent for me to be accepted for honours. This sounded so trivial in my head. I went to one of my prayer warriors(a prayer partner) and told her about the pickle I was in. I felt a calling to do my honours that year, but even Rhodes University had declined me and I had no backup plan. Here is another good example of yielding to God's plan over your life. I knew He called me to do my honours. Though I had been overconfident in my results and only applied to one university, I knew God's plan would come to pass. I still needed to put in the work and reach out to universities that would allow late applications. My prayer warrior and I prayed, and after prayer I called every university in the country. The University of KwaZulu Natal (UKZN) responded favourably and as I would have it that week, they were taking late applications, but only in person. So, I went and I got in. At this point I was not very picky about what honours programme I got into. If I am being honest, much of our education journey is cemented in our undergraduate, in the first two years of our degree career. The last year is honestly spent building very little on concepts from first and second year.

I have always felt my destiny being highly connected to the person I would marry since I was a little girl. All those who know me personally will tell you how I always talk about the love of my life. For me it's less about the romantic side, though that is very important too. It's understanding two destinies tied and sealed by God. This is the very same area that has been under constant attack from the enemy in my life. See, I honestly have no problem attracting men to my life. I used to think this was cool and a blessing, until I grew in my spiritual life. I realised that the area God wants to use you in, the area of your greatest anointing, is also the very same area the enemy will attack and use as your Achilles' heel.

I knew going to UKZN was a journey of purpose for me. I actually told myself I would use the year to draw close to God and not date. I tell you, the minute I arrived in UKZN I had a sea, no, an ocean of boys around me. Much of this though, I believe, is the novelty of someone and something new. I was invited to football games in Durban, all the way from Pietermaritzburg, before I even knew how to get to class. In hindsight, I should have been aware that the enemy was at play. A week later I met a gentleman whom I'd later marry. This is an area of my life I had not fully surrendered to God, but I was deeply aware that I needed to. When I met my ex-husband on my way to gym on campus, I prayed about it.

I was walking around campus trying to find the gym, when I saw two gentlemen in gym clothes. So, I stopped them and asked if I could walk with them to the gym. They agreed and we starting talking along the way. When we got to the gym, JJ, my ex-husband, noticed my disappointment with the facilities. So, he gave me his number and said he would be happy to show me other gyms around town not too far from campus if I was interested. I went home and prayed that evening. Make no mistake, I am fully aware of my alluring nature. I prayed to God that if this is not the person He wants me to connect with, then He must show me. Show me God did, but I ignored every red flag there was. I instead thought it was a carnival. I called JJ the next day and we went around the city and looked at all gyms, comparing facilities and prices.

I ended up using the campus one and we went to gym together. I only met one other person that year apart from JJ. I spent most of my time with JJ. I was drawn to him because he was so different from all the guys I had ever liked. Ours was not an instantaneous or deep connection. In fact, there were elements of rejection that drew me closer to him. I remember telling him about my abortion, and I will never forget the look on his face. Red flag number one. JJ was a pious man. He kept the Sabbath and prayed like no man I'd ever known before. I was still on my journey of coming back to Jesus, and he represented something I wanted and thought I needed in my life at the time. When I told him I had an abortion, I felt the rejection and disdain in his voice. He said something I'll never forget.

"I am so glad you did not keep the baby."

This cut me to the core because this was not a decision I came to lightly. I felt misunderstood by him. My spirit told me not to, but the power of rejection forced me to stay and gain his acceptance and approval.

JJ and I dated for the rest of the year and walked our devout lives together. JJ was walking with a 'woman of God.' I never told him about my past, my toxic behaviour, or my previous relationships with men. I hid this part of my life well, and it was easy to do so because I was in a new city and none of my old friends from UCT where there. I only introduced my prayer warriors to JJ. Boy, oh boy, God is funny. The next year we moved to Johannesburg together. I had received an investment banking job with HSBC and he was on the final round of interviews with Absa bank. In my head, we were going to be the young power couple taking over Johannesburg.

JJ was rejected by Absa bank and I found myself the breadwinner in the relationship. This completely shifted the dynamics in our relationship. In UKZN, JJ had the financial upper hand. He came from a wealthy family and was not from South Africa, so his parents sent him way more money than he needed. He had a car too, or at least access to one. Now we found ourselves in Johannesburg relying on me financially. When JJ did not get the job with Absa, his parents told him to go back home and not stay in

Johannesburg. If he chose to stay, they would cut him off financially. Red flag number two. God is a God of process, authority and obedience. Did JJ and I listen to his parents? No, we did not. JJ stayed in Johannesburg with me. We shared a tiny apartment. Year one went by without JJ getting a job. I saw him sink deeply into depression. I saw a man who had given up completely on his dreams. He stopped applying for jobs, stopped eating, and was so angry.

I came home one day and found him a little bit happier. I inquired about the sudden change in his mood. He told me he had figured out the reason for not getting a job: it was because he did not have a work permit. So, I asked how he could get one. He said the easiest way was through marriage. It did not immediately jump to me that we should get married.

I said, "Okay," and went about my life.

If I am being honest, I had had it up to the ceiling at this stage with JJ's unemployment. I had taken over the burden of submitting applications for him. At work, I would use my lunch time to submit job applications on his behalf. Before I get to how we decided marriage was the best route to take, I need to explain our different personalities.

This is something the gift of hindsight has allowed me to see clearly and understand. JJ is a very creative thinker and a visionary. One of those personalities that will probably come up with solutions to problems we didn't even know we have. He applied a backward induction in his idea of marriage.

He thought, "I am going to marry this lady in the future, and in the now, marriage is a very creative solution to this problem we are facing."

I believe this deep in my heart to be the case. He was committing to a forever in the present. Now, here comes the issue of differences in personalities and opinions. I, on the other hand, am a very pragmatic personality. I saw marriage as a solution to the present problem and absolutely not the future. I remember seeking counsel from a friend on this issue. Well, not counsel, but rather seeking a witness. She asked me if JJ was the guy I saw in my future, as he was so different from what I liked and was usually attracted to. I said that if I was being honest, I was plagued by confusion and was struggling to see the future. But if things did not work out, I would divorce him. I went back to my apartment and I told JJ he could look into this marriage work permit thing and that I was happy to do it. In my head it was solving a now situation. I thought that all our problems and relationship issues that had piled up at this point were a result of his unemployment. JJ had managed to blame everything on his unemployment. He no longer took me out because he was unemployed. He no longer dressed well or went to gym because he was saving money. Not that I believed all of this, but at this point I was curious to see if the person I had fallen in love with, whatever I knew and understood love to be, would resurface if this issue of money was eliminated. I forgot a basic concept. A problem, or rather how one handles a problem, only reveals their character. It never forces them to behave in a manner outside of who they are. This is a lesson I would be reminded of immediately after I divorced JJ five years later.

JJ and I had been going to church. But at this point in time, it was merely a Sunday activity. Neither one of us was learning or seeking God. We sought counsel from our pastor, who failed us dismally.

He said, "Oh well, if you are both sure and see it as a solution then I am happy to arrange it here at church so you at least don't have to go to the magistrate's office."

I was extremely uncomfortable with the idea of going to the magistrate. If I was going to betray myself and God, it had to be in a place I at least thought God would be present in.

The wedding day came. My mother was in town visiting and JJ's parents were also in town for a scheduled hospital procedure. We sat them down and told them of our plans to get married. It had now been two going on three years of JJ being unemployed. We made a compelling argument. We knew we would get married one day, so why not now if it meant JJ would get a job? See, while JJ was transparent with both his parents, I was strategic about the parent I involved at this stage. I only told my mother because, for all the years I've known my mother, she is not disciplinary. I don't remember my mother ever refusing me on big issues. She will stand firm when it comes to me not going to the gym, because only men go to the gym. But where it matters the most, it never came. Even when I wished she would. I did not tell my dad because he would have refused. No not necessarily because of my wellbeing, but, I believe, because of tradition and him wanting lobola first. See, I have come to understand that God is a God of process. He implements His will through people, sometimes even through the people that will oppose you at times. And it's up to us to hear His voice and discern when opposition is of God and when it is not.

I was not excited at all on the day of my 'wedding.' I

could not even bring myself to at least go get a nice dress for the pictures. I had this nagging feeling that I was making the biggest mistake of my life. I kept looking at JJ, hoping he would sense my spirit and we would agree to back out.

I never really considered myself a people-pleaser but I looked around that day and found myself not wanting to let anyone down by saying, "Hey, look, I think I moved well ahead of myself here."

I had no idea when I told JJ to look into the marriage thing that his father would be sick and have to come to the city and that my mother would also be in town the very same weekend we had scheduled our pastor to officiate our marriage.

I talked myself into believing it was just wedding jitters and that I'd get over it in time. They say a kiss is often the most passionate act in a relationship. I never felt any passion kissing JJ, and it was heavily cemented on our wedding day. I felt a coldness and emptiness during the kiss. I knew I had betrayed myself and all things romantic I had ever believed in. We went for a celebratory lunch afterwards. I could not even eat. I believe I low-key resented JJ for being so happy and not picking up my nonverbal cues, even during the lunch. His inability to pick up my non-verbal cues would plague our relationship for years to come.

The parents went home, and JJ and I were left to resume our life. Our 'happily never after.' Up until the day we divorced, I never told other members of my family I was married. Others found out through word of mouth. The same was true of some of JJ's family members who did not attend the wedding. My five years of marriage to JJ showed me that God truly never forsakes you. He is able to use even your worst mistake and work it into something for your good. I believe God took a back seat because I never surrendered this relationship to Him. It was honestly a fear-based relationship from the get-go. Fear of being rejected from when I told him about the abortion. Fear of not being able to provide financially if we did not take matters into our own hands. In the five years I was married to JJ, it was like God had now decided to intervene and would show Himself to me in strange ways.

I suppose I was now able to trust my intuition because I was also growing in my relationship with God. I remember one of JJ's best friends was getting married. He was so in love with his wife that he wanted to propose with the best engagement ring. Here was God revealing that masculine energy I find so endearing and attractive in a man. He asked JJ and I to go look for a ring at Browns in Sandton. He was based in Malawi and could not come to the country himself. JJ and I went to Brown's as instructed. Let's go back a little here. Remember JJ had been unemployed and financially cut off by his parents. JJ never proposed to me. He pitched marriage as a solution to his unemployment problem and I happily participated. Now that you are reminded of this, let's go back to Browns.

JJ's friend had just starting working in Malawi. My pragmatic self did not imagine him having a huge budget for this ring, and JJ never shared the budget. Maybe I just never asked and went along with my assumptions. JJ's friend was going to propose to the daughter of one of the wealthiest men in Malawi. We got to Browns, and I saw a nice ring within the budget I had in my head. I showed JJ and told him I thought it was nice and well within budget. He asked me how much it was. It was under R10 000. JJ looked at me and said how dare I think that was worthy for Mpimpi's daughter, Mpimpi being the wealthy father. I looked at him with utter shock. I vividly remember feeling God speaking to me strongly. I was so upset. Actually, that's not the correct word. I was livid. How dare he know the value of money or speak of worth when he had the audacity to marry me without a proposal? Without even paying lobola. Yes, I was reverting back to tradition. I asked him where my worth was when he thought it was a good idea to marry me without an engagement ring? Where was my worth when we decided on a chapel wedding?

It dawned on me for the first time how I had sold myself short. I stormed out of Browns actually more upset with myself than JJ. See, in my head, I saw JJ's idea of us getting married from a practical perspective. I did not even realise that he thought of marriage and proposals from this angle. If he did, where was this thinking when it came to us? For the very first time, I re-examined the whole thing and looked at it from a value perspective. It completely unnerved me and my feelings of self-betrayal came rushing back like a gust of wind. However, at this point I had grown on my Christian journey, and with years also piling up the magnitude of the decision I had taken was hitting me hard. I was now deeply aware of the consequences of a decision I had made at twenty-one years of age. The idea of divorce came back into my mind. But I managed to supress it.

As if God was trying to show me that He was never in this from the beginning, people from my past and friendships I had abandoned came back into my life. I have learned that every time God is about to do something in your life, He starts by shifting relationships, removing people from your life and bringing in those who will do His bidding. When I was not out of the country travelling by myself, I started going out a lot. I had resumed my heavy drinking. I would sometimes blackout and come back home drunk. I started buying wine and drinking a bottle to go to sleep. I noticed JJ's disdain every time I got drunk. I think this low-key motivated me to continue.

I managed my dysfunction and never missed a day at work. I got to the office and found an email from one of the applications I had submitted on behalf of JJ. They wanted to see him. I told him and he went for the job interview. I had made so many excuses for JJ. I managed to blame the whole incident that took place at Browns on his unemployment. Yes, I did. We were now well into year three or four of our marriage and JJ still had no job. All our fights revolved around him staying home all day and not cleaning or cooking or even applying for any jobs. I remember coming home one day and finding dirty dishes. JJ had been on the couch the whole day. I walked in and asked him how many job applications had he submitted that day, knowing very well what the answer was because it was down to me on the application front. Not only was I working a demanding job, I had also enrolled for my master's degree, and to come home and be expected to clean after JJ and cook for him was the straw that broke this camel's back. Seeing those dirty dishes and his cavalier responses to me, I snapped. My idea of snapping is going absolutely silent and sometimes disappearing, something that annoyed JJ. I went to our room and ignored him while he was talking to me about the many great business ideas that had become the norm for him.

He marched in after me and continued talking. I pulled up my phone and ignored him. In my head, JJ was going to take the internship whether he liked it or not and I did not care to hear of any business idea he had.

He snapped and took my phone and threw it at the wall. He flipped the bed upside down and broke the bedroom window. I left home and booked myself into a hotel. I got a call from JJ hours later telling me he was about to commit suicide if I didn't come back home. I did not believe, not even one bit, that he would. For all I know on this topic, people who are serious about committing suicide do not make announcements. At the very best, they leave a note. But I thought that if anything happened to him and I ignored his call for help, I would never be able to forgive myself. So, I went back home. He had taken a couple of pain killers. I asked our neighbours to help me put him in the car. I took him to the hospital. The doctor said they would pump his stomach, but the dosage was not enough to cause any serious harm. She asked if he suffered from any mental health problems or came from a family with a history of mental health issues. I could not answer this, as I too did not know. I am a believer in discretion and keeping things between those who strictly need to know. JJ begged me not to tell his parents or mine. But I knew I had to at least tell his family so I could establish if they had a history of mental health problems. I called his parents. They confirmed they did have a history of mental health issues and assured me they would speak to JJ.

Being the thinker that I am, I forced myself to re-examine the whole situation and look at it holistically. I came to the conclusion it was not working for me. Being the Christian and God-loving person I am, I was so scared of being the initiator of divorce. I went back to our apartment after spending a day at the hotel I had already paid for and taking the break I knew I needed. I asked JJ if our relationship had been working for him. He said it was. He never asked me how I was. JJ was never one to pick up my verbal or non-verbal cues at all. I don't think he realised the motions for divorce had begun in my head. He assured me he would go to therapy and seek help. I asked for a three-month trial separation to see how we would function without each other. I moved into an apartment five minutes away. Not the best idea at all. JJ was in my apartment every day and basically moved in.

I saw running two household as wasteful, so I moved out of my new apartment and back with JJ before the three months even ended. His sister, who lived in Italy, was getting married, and we were asked to be part of the bridal party. In our four years of marriage, JJ had never agreed to travel with me anywhere. I was shocked that we were even going to his sister's wedding. Ever the strategic thinker, I saw this as an opportunity to finally see what travelling with JJ would be like. I told him that if I was paying for myself to go to Italy for a wedding, I was going to make it a holiday too. He agreed. One of JJ's qualities that I liked and admired at times was his love for his family. I found it perplexing though, as he could never really extend that same love to others. For me, I believe some things should be universal.

It makes no sense to claim to love God and your family, but refuse to love others, even to love your own wife in the manner she wants to be loved.

JJ and I planned our holiday to Italy. I left most of the details to him as he was quite good at it. This was a decision I would later regret. See, in my head there were obvious activities in each city we had agreed to go to that couples should do together. It never crossed my mind to explicitly communicate this to JJ. The trip to Italy was my equivalent to Paul's Road to Damascus. As if I was not already aware of our marital problems and huge differences, the trip would reveal all of it. When we got to Italy, we landed in Rome and decided to make Rome our starting city. We fought over everything. In my marriage to JJ, it would be easier to count the moments we did not fight than the ones we did. But the pinnacle of the fighting was in Rome and Venice. In Rome, we had gone out for supper. We got into a huge argument, to the point he thought it was a good idea to leave me alone in a restaurant. I had to find my way back to the Airbnb by myself.

My energy levels were already highly tested at this stage. Ever the optimist, I kept believing or hoping we would see eye to eye on this trip. That it might even be the trip that brings us closer together. We arrived in Venice and the only activity I was interested in and assumed JJ had arranged or considered was the Gondola ride. Not only had JJ not considered or booked it, even after I explained to him the significance it had and why I wanted to get on it, he was not moved an inch. I remember him saying we would come back for it one day. I told him I would be coming back but not with him. These had become familiar statements from my side, as I no longer saw a future with JJ. While our end vision aligned, which pulled us together in the first place, our ideas of getting there proved to be fundamentally different. Our youth did not help either. JJ was only a year older than me. We were ill equipped for the journey we had entered on a whim. We were both very stubborn and failed dismally at the art of compromise.

We got back to South Africa, and divorce had been set firm in my heart. I spoke to JJ about it and he told me he would never divorce me. He told me that divorce was not an option for him, that he entered the marriage with forever, and that he would only divorce me if I committed adultery. A seed was once again planted in my heart. I stayed in the marriage with JJ and was committed to him and it. It never crossed my mind to cheat on him until a real opportunity to presented itself and I would find myself revisiting this conversation.

On year five of our marriage, 2019, friends I had made during my trip to Russia were in the country. I was so happy to reunite with them. I was excited for JJ to finally meet people I had connected with during my solo trips. This is a year I had begun a venture with a friend of hosting salon-style dinners, where we would invite people around and discuss pressing issues of the day. I told JJ about this venture and he shut it down. He was so unsupportive. In an effort to show me his disapproval he never attended any of our dinners. He even refused to attend the launch. My friends from Russia invited me and JJ to a party they were hosting in their mansion in Sandhurst. JJ refused to attend, so I went by myself. I was back to my heavy drinking again. At the braai, I met Haysus. Our energies connected instantaneously. I spent a lot of time with Haysus. I never imagined either of us would act on our desire as we were both married. This gave me a false sense of security around Haysus. Nothing happened at the party. I drove back home drunk from Russian vodka.

I found myself hanging at this house a lot. I started even lying to JJ about my whereabouts. At this point I did not want him to meet my friends. The house had become my little escape. All of a sudden, JJ took a keen interest in meeting my friends. Meanwhile, my bond with Haysus was growing. Haysus came to the launch of our dinner talk, the idea my own husband would not support. Haysus enjoyed it and thought it was a brilliant idea. I never directly invited Haysus. I had invited my good friend from the house; she could not make it, and shared the invitation in the house. Haysus and two others came.

We went out for dinners with the guys. We were just exploring Joburg and doing activities together, which JJ took no interest in. See, amongst our many differences, JJ is highly introverted and I am an extrovert. Not to the extreme though, hence why I believe we co-existed well together in some parts. I also have no doubt that our faith, and his commitment to seeing things to the end no matter what, kept us together longer than most. I must admit I too did not understand JJ fully. I had no grace for him. I did not know how to protect his insecurities. In fact, I believe I did a spectacular job at exposing them.

There were moments where I should have stopped and perhaps stayed at home with him, not for nothing but to make him feel protected and validated in his insecurities. But, like he did with me, I did not pick up JJ's uncommunicated and non-verbal cues. I knew he was introverted, but it never crossed my mind, not even once, to ask how he felt about me forcing him to attend social gatherings with strangers where we would indulge in behaviours he detested and frankly judged. I also know I did not ask because at this stage I felt depleted, and could not give any more in the name of JJ. I was extremely selfish at this stage and did anything I wanted, how I wanted and when I wanted to. I lost respect for JJ years ago. I was merely tolerating him by now. For three years we had no intimacy. I went from tolerating his kisses to completely refusing to kiss him.

We went to couples therapy separately. I am not entirely sure what JJ's discussions were or if he even went. I remember asking him, and I got a strong sense he was not going to his sessions. Instead, he started talking a lot about his personal assistant in whom he had found a listening ear. In 2018, JJ's company where he was interning had been bought by a huge consulting firm. He got promoted and even got a PA. I, on the other hand, was working through the idea of divorce with my therapist. In the years of his unemployment, JJ believed he had perfected a business idea, which his PA now fully supported. In June of 2019, he resigned from his job to pursue the business venture. He told his PA of this decision, and never shared it with me until his last day of serving his notice. When I asked him why he could not tell me this in the beginning, given his mind was already set and my voice would obviously not stop him, he dismissed me and shrugged. At this point, I saw no reason for us to continue being married if he felt comfortable discussing huge family matters with is PA instead of me.

I went out that night to go see Haysus. Yes, I left the house knowing if Haysus made any move I would not stop him at all. I got to Haysus' place, and we ate and talked and drank vodka. This time I did not stop Haysus. I never regretted having sex with Haysus per se, but my cowardice in not just ending my marriage and allowing things to get ugly and messy and complicated is what tore me up the most. It hit me when I got home and found JJ pacing up and down the house waiting for me at two a.m. that what I had done was flip the blame all on me. I had invited a distraction from our already existing problems. He did not need to ask me to know something had finally happened this time. I played out many scenarios during my drive home, and I could have never imagined what was to unfold.

The very same JJ who had asked me not to tell anyone about his suicide attempt and him physically hitting me with a double bed, called all of my family members and his and told them I had cheated on him. He called our pastor too. Anyone who would listen he told. I felt humiliated, exposed and naked. I myself had not even wrapped my head around what I had done. I was in shock. You see, I am a very loyal person. Despite how I entered the marriage to JJ, I tried my best to stay committed until the very end. In sleeping with Haysus I not only betrayed God, but I betrayed myself, my values and my faith once again.

I asked JJ for a divorce again and he refused. He told me he loved me and was still committed to us. He invited our pastor every day, but told him half-truths. I continued with my therapist, who really did a phenomenal job in helping me see what was my fault and what was not. At this point, all of JJ's family had placed the blame with me because I cheated. My own mother I believe blamed me to some degree. The narrative circulating on both sides of the family was that I had committed adultery. After one of our pastoral sessions arranged solely by JJ, he told me he was confident he would be able to forgive me. Not now, but one day.

I found it awfully impressive that JJ was the one moving along like a trooper and coming up with solutions. I was still in shock, and could not think properly. I could not believe what I had done. Anyone who met me between 2019 and 2020 will tell you I was still talking about me committing adultery and how my marriage had ended because I committed adultery. This was absolutely not the case but JJ's handling of the situation, including our families' reactions, cemented in me an enormous amount of guilt.

I found myself once again in trouble. I knew I had to run to God and isolate myself from everyone and everything. I leaned into my faith. I read the Bible like I never read it before. I took time out to pray and went on a trip to Tanzania to find myself, or rather, to hear God. I realised that whatever had happened, my marriage no longer represented the love of God. I remember having a sobering conversation with a friend before departing for Tanzania, and I told her for the first time everything that had happened in my marriage. Her response was that if that was what marriage was all about, she didn't want it. It cut me deep. I knew I had a heavy hand in creating an institution that absolutely did not resemble the love of God and how

He wanted marriage to be. It is when I eventually got to this realisation that I felt confident in my decision to get a divorce.

Divorces are complicated, and often take time. Granted, JJ did not contest mine when I filed. It was approved within a week. This was such a confirmation that I had made the right decision. I chose to seek forgiveness from God, rather than from JJ. Not for nothing I knew I would spend the rest of my life trying to prove my repentance to JJ. Prior to me filing for divorce and going on my mission to Tanzania, JJ had forbidden me from seeing my Russian friends ever. He forced me to delete Haysus' number, which I did not. I merely changed his name. I never saw any possibility of a relationship with Haysus. I was not interested in any, for that matter. I knew I would delete his number eventually, but I just hated being forced to by JJ. I felt he expected me to have no feelings about what happened, because, in his eyes, I was guilty and committed this sin. I was not allowed to feel anything. Not even once did JJ ever ask me how I felt about the whole thing. He never sat down with me to discuss what I thought was the best way to handle everything. For me, this cemented how the nature of his 'forgiveness' would go for the rest of our lives. That I would forever have to do what he wants at my expense. While he had every right to be upset, and I will forever be sorry for what I did to him, I knew I could not live a life of bondage over this. I admit, I don't know how things would have played out if I chose to stay, but I know my marriage was nothing to fight for at that point.

I firmly believe JJ and I lasted for that long because of God's mercy and love for both of us. My marriage taught me things I would have never learned anywhere else. It revealed my character flaws, how much I still needed to learn about who God is and how He loves. I entered my marriage for what I knew love to be in a human way and what I saw modelled in front of me. It took me being in that marriage to see what love is not. The very first church service I went to after my divorce was finalised, they were talking about what it means when God tells a man to love his wife as God loves the church. This is not the same church I went to with JJ. The pastor used practical examples of how, if you love your wife and she wants to go out, you will do it. Even if you do not want to at the very least, it makes her happy. Of course, there is a balance to be reached where one spouse is not always bending to the point that they compromise who they are.

There is no concept and no one more misunderstood than Jesus. I often look back at my marriage to JJ and wonder how two people who claimed to love Jesus got it so wrong when it came to loving each other. Multiple factors were at play which countered against us, such as our age, lack of wider family support, and our differences in how we gave and received love. The most important challenge we faced, I believe, is our deeply flawed understanding of the love of God and who God is. At this point, you might wonder why I do not count finances. From my experience, I shrug every time someone says their relationship failed because of finances. I deeply believe finance masks a deeper problem. JJ never proposed to me or bought me a ring, not because he was unemployed, but because he did not want to. Rings go for as little as R200 from second-hand shops, even the local pharmacy. Yes, I would have accepted that ring, because I understood JJ's predicament. Heck, I even married him without the ring. As for not going out for dates and holidays, JJ simply did not value going out or travelling. We went to Italy for his sister's wedding despite all of his financial challenges. Without fail, every summer holidays JJ and I travelled to Malawi to see his family. I believe that where there is a will there will absolutely be a way.

Our flawed love and understanding of who God is and the reckless love He has for us was important. Firstly, you can never be able to truly love someone if you have never received love yourself. Never mind experiencing unconditional love. While most of the time our parents love us and even claim to do so unconditionally, it unfortunately sometimes comes with conditions, whether fully expressed or not. You notice it from a very young age. For example, when you come home on time and your mother is happy with you. When you do well at school, and you get all the Christmas gifts on your list. This is modelling the idea that you need to earn love. I am sorry, but I must admit that some churches also do not do a great job at modelling and translating God's reckless love either. Any believer who delegates their obligation to seek and know who God is to a preacher is doing themselves a great disservice. The best understanding of God's love comes from having a personal relationship with Him. Like any relationship, you need to invest time and resources to it. You need to read His word and spend time meditating on it. You need to surround yourself with people who have had personal encounters with God, whether it's through attending conferences or reading their books. God is still a God of miracles. The God who is able to heal the paralysed. Unfortunately, these kinds of stories are hard to hear these days, as media platforms have become hostile to things witnessed without evidence. But if you seek people's stories, you will hear about such wonders. As I will also share in the chapters to come.

I am often asked if I regret marrying JJ. I am not one who believes in regrets. I believe God is able to work even your worst mistakes for your good. I do not regret marrying JJ, not one bit. Do I wish we could have done things differently? Yes. Do I wish we had waited? Absolutely. Time only reveals the truth. Had we given ourselves time, it would have revealed to us that the problems JJ and I had were not financial, but character flaws that needed to be worked out. The latter brings me to why I can never regret my marriage. It did a work on my character that I would have never learned from 'dating.' I needed to be in that battlefield to unmask my flaws and work on them. I absolutely believe my last husband will be a lucky man. Not only will he benefit from my awesomeness, but he will get a wife who has gained first-hand experience on the battlefield of marriage. I thank God that both JJ and I grew into better versions of ourselves, and never changed who we were to please the other. This is how I knew our journey had reached the end. It hit me during one of my counselling sessions that at the core I was asking JJ to be someone he was not, and he was expecting me to be someone I was not either. I also did not allow my marriage to stop me from pursuing my dreams. I went after every opportunity that came to me, and JJ pursued his dreams as well. For these reasons I do not regret it at all, and I do not believe it was time wasted. I believe it saved me from a litany of boyfriends and heartbreaks. Also, God is a restorer of time. Whatever time I may have lost in the spiritual and actual realm, I know He will restore tenfold. I planted a seed in my marriage with JJ that I will reap in my next relationship.

The Eye of the Storm

In November 2019, my divorce to JJ was approved. I was officially a 'divorcee.' I wish I could blame all my challenges on the pandemic and write to you that all my challenges started in 2020. My storm was already in motion in 2019. In December of 2019, I met a prophet who gave me a prophecy. I was due to fly to my already-booked holiday in Zanzibar. She begged me to cancel the trip and not go. This was like a day to two before my flight was scheduled to depart. This was the second time in my life I had ever received a prophecy. The first time I was about five years old, and had gone with my dad to visit his friend. A lady saw me and told me I would get my first job at a very young age. She was not an acclaimed prophet. Also, the wording I felt was quite broad, and applicable to almost anyone. I never thought about it ever again, for the most part.

However, this prophecy was much more specific to my life. It touched parts of my soul and things God had already placed in my heart. Also, I was much older and more seasoned in my Christian walk. I could not ignore it. The next day, I went to one of my prayer warriors, and she shared with me her views and thoughts on prophecies. We prayed like never before and agreed I would step out in faith and proceed with my trip. I am not one to ever put up my hand at church to receive a prophecy. Not for my lack of belief in it, but because more than anything I believe once you hear something it cannot be unheard.

I went to Zanzibar. I forgot about the prophecy until New Year's Eve. I had invited a good friend of mine to come with me on the trip. We spent New Year's Eve at the Kwenda Rocks hotel, a five-star hotel. They hosted a full moon party that evening. My friend and I had made new friends and we were popping champagne. We drank from the morning until two a.m. when the party ended. Stumbling, we made our way to our room. We had to go through the hotel reception to get to our room. I remember my friend being dramatic at reception and drawing attention to herself. She was actually trying to smuggle a friend we met in Zanzibar to our room. While waiting for them, I saw there was a very handsome tall Indian man at reception. I was still in my bikini from the morning of the previous day. He walked towards me, and I jumped right into his arms. He caught me and took me to his room. I thought he was taking me to my room. I realised we were headed the wrong way when I started not recognising the way. I started screaming and yelling. Starting to sober up I kicked and punched, but he overpowered me. We got to his room, and he threw me on the bed and took off my bikini bottom. As he was about to penetrate me, I shouted that I had HIV, or something to do with HIV. He backed up and went to look for a condom. I ran for the door and left everything behind.

My brain on full alert, I remembered the way back to my room and told my friends what had happened. We waited for the sun to come up and went to report the incident to hotel management. The management team did nothing, and refused to give us a hotel shuttle to go to the hospital. We had to use our resources to find a hospital that was two hours away. We got to the hospital and received the warmest of treatment. When I told the doctor what happened, he did not seem shocked at all. I would later find out that such instances occur quite often on the island, especially to young black females travelling by themselves. He put me on emergency HIV treatment just in case. We still had a week left of the holiday. My friend offered to end the holiday and go home with me. This made absolutely no sense in my head.

I was walking with a peace that surpasses all understanding. I knew my prayers were not in vain. What I did not know back then, which I do know now, is that the minute you receive a prophecy, you should prepare yourself for the battle of your life. But have no fear, because absolutely no weapon formed against you shall prosper. We finished our holiday and returned to South Africa. When I got home, I realised the sealed packet of Preventative HIV pills I was taking was missing ten pills. The emergency treatment was meant to be twenty-eight days. I called my doctor and went in to see him. He told me they didn't have those kinds of pills, and I would have to continue the treatment with the same pills I began with. He told me he doubted anywhere in the country had the kind I needed, because the government had discontinued them. I went home and had a cup of tea, thinking that was just my luck.

In 2018, I was working on project where I had to map all government clinics in Gauteng, and had gone to visit each of them to get a programme going in the areas. I pulled out my documents and called the clinics. One of the clinics in Alexander had the pills in storage. I went to the clinic and told the nurse what had happened. She was so sympathetic and did everything to retrieve the pills from storage. If you're familiar with government processes, you'll know this was not a particularly easy task. She gave me the ten pills I needed. I went home and told the friend I had travelled with about the mix-up from Zanzibar and how I managed to find the additional ten.

For me, this demonstrated again the power of God in our lives. The reckless love He has for those who call on Him. Left to my doctor's advice, I would have accepted that nothing could be done, as according to him the pills had been discontinued. What he had no idea of was that he was talking to lady of faith who believes in the impossible. I knew there was no way my God would play tricks with me like this. I also became very sensitive to the prophecy I received. I thought that if hell was unleashing its demons, then there must be some truth, maybe even a lot of truth, to the word I received. When I say hell unleashed demons, I am specifically talking about the sealed pack of pills missing ten pills. I absolutely do not absolve myself of the decisions I made. Decisions have consequences. I decided to drink the whole day. I decided to jump into the arms of a stranger, and unfortunately those decisions had consequences.

I reached out to the prophet to let her know all that happened and to thank her. I absolutely would not have covered my travels with as much prayer had she not spoken to me. Little did I know, this was just the beginning. We met up for lunch and she had more to give me. I went home feeling that I was about to enter the deepest spiritual battle of my life. It was now January of 2020, with a looming pandemic ahead. I was working for the South African Federation of Trade Unions as Economic Researcher and Policy Manager. I had moved in with the friend I travelled to Zanzibar with. The move was an opportunity that came up, and I thought I could benefit from the company of a housemate while I eased into single life. She was also going through a divorce. This meant I had a friend who could actually understand everything I was going through. Talking about my divorce was strange to a lot of my friends. At their cores, they just simply could not understand or relate to it. Many of them were on the other side of the spectrum, believing and praying for marriage, and here I was talking about being divorced.

In January of 2020, my job stopped paying my salary. I was the first one to return to the office after my holiday from hell. I got to the office, and it was me and the receptionist who were back. She said my research assistant would be back in two days, and she would not come in on some days. Out of all the jobs I had, I truly enjoyed this one. It brought out the best parts of me and utilised the best components of my personality. On the day the research assistant came back, I got to the office, went straight into my office and locked it. I never locked my door before. But that day I went in and locked myself in, never to come out until it was time to go home. I never even went to the toilet. I thought this was strange, as I drank nothing less than two litres of water a day. On my way home, I bumped into my research assistant at reception. He greeted me and asked why I had

63

locked myself in my office. I remember looking at him and getting a sense of disdain. I felt that, given the chance, this guy would hurt me. I do not think I gave him an answer, and reached for the door and went home.

The next morning, I woke up, went to gym, and literally had no energy for work. Something like this had never happened. I thought to myself that if I did not go in my boss would never know, as he would only be back in a week's time. But I felt like I was cheating. Facing a moral dilemma, I decided not to go in. I didn't go to the office that week, until my boss came back a day early. He called me around ten a.m. and asked where I was, as he was in the office, and I was not there. I told him I was on the way and that I had gotten stuck on the train. I literally jumped on the next bus and headed to work. The Gaubus and train moved at lightning-speed. I made it downtown and was at the office by eleven-thirty a.m. Everyone seemed to have been alerted that my boss, the head of the organisation, was returning that day. We all gathered at his office. My late arrival did not faze him. He told us that, before Christmas the previous year, he had received "intelligence" that my research assistant had rape allegations in North West Province (a different province) and had an ongoing trial. He looked at me and apologised for not letting me know sooner, knowing I would be the first in the office with the research assistant. He also informed me that his type of victim were young educated light skinned girls. I fit this description on the dot. My boss assured me they would handle the matter and fire the research assistant, and they did.

My energy levels were seriously diminishing at this stage. At the end of the month, when my salary did not come in, I reached boiling point. I called my boss to inquire about this, and he gave me the run around. He then offered to "loan" me some cash. Imagine that, working and not getting paid. Instead, you get offered a loan for your own salary. It is important to give context at this stage. My position at the federation was a donor-sponsored job. My salary was actually coming from the donor and not the federation. I was the highest paid person in the organization. My boss felt entitled to take my salary and misuse it because I was young and, in his mind, I had no real obligations. Also, the federation was not doing well financially at all.

I felt cornered. Bills were looming and I was not financially prepared for this mess at work. I decided to take my boss up on his loan offer. I asked him to wire the loan into my bank account. He told me he couldn't, as his account was in the negative. He said I needed to go fetch the money in person. I told my roommate and told her this was dodgy to the core. She told me to go fetch the cash at his house and use an Uber. She told me to make sure the Uber driver waited for me, and that she would keep count of how long I was gone for and call me if she started to panic. I did as we planned and went. Honestly, I was in a state of deep confusion. I still had not fully recovered from Zanzibar, my assistant, and now this.

I got to my boss' house and his whole family was there. I immediately relaxed and waited for him to go retrieve the cash in his bedroom. I took the brown envelope and left. I felt a combination of disbelief, numbness, and confusion. I would remain in this state for the next two years. I decided to quit my job. I was unemployed, and dealing with my divorce, Zanzibar, and everything that had happened at work. Nothing in me said to stop, pause, reset, and reflect. I continued with life. I shared what had happened at work with a colleague of mine, and he connected me with a consulting gig for an international NGO. I joined the NGO the very next month. I left the NGO and took on other consulting work for the rest of the year. After my divorce, my bank balance at the end of 2019 was zero, and my savings account was reduced to about R80 000. At the end of 2020, God had multiplied my savings by a factor of three, and continued to show up in my finances throughout 2021 during a pandemic.

However, emotionally, and spiritually I was depleted. My depletion hit me towards the end of 2020, when I started forgetting things. I would go to a restaurant with friends and forget to pay the bill. I knew this was strange behaviour and out of character. The pandemic added an additional layer of disorientation in my life. I went for virtual therapy, and it did not help me at all. I spent time in prayer and seeking God, but honestly, I slept throughout most of the pandemic in 2020. When the opportunity came, I found ways to distract myself. I was still drinking, but not as much, largely due to the restrictions imposed by the government on the sale of alcohol. My roommate moved back home for the whole of 2020, and I was quarantined by myself. I tried to use the time to reflect on everything that had happened and was happening. Nothing in me said to stop and seek professional help. I felt extremely tired all the time.

In February of 2021, after praying and consulting God,

I decided to leave Johannesburg and move in with a friend in Cape Town. I sincerely prayed about this move as I understood the importance of being planted in the right environment, especially at this critical age. Despite my fasting and prayer, I still felt God was silent. One thing I knew was that my income stream had dried up in Johannesburg. I had worked myself to the bone to try and replenish my savings, and I was not going to stay in Johannesburg and maintain my life like I was employed. This was something I had done very often in the past, which was part of why I had so little savings after my divorce.

I moved in with a friend in March 2021 and stayed with her until June the same year. If I thought my life was dramatic in Johannesburg, Cape Town was about to show me how much worse things could get. Cape Town was hard because of the length of time in which everything happened. In Johannesburg, for the most part things happened over time and gradually. My divorce was the hardest mountain I had to overcome, because of the nature of intimacy and proximity. I arrived in Cape Town March of 2021 and by the end of the month I was in a relationship with Ben. I remember having a conversation with Ben and us agreeing the timing was terrible. But we continued, nonetheless. I felt comfortable to proceed with the relationship because I had known Ben for a long time. We went to UCT together and he was best friends with the friend I moved in with. He felt safe. The is a common thread here I should highlight. I chose JJ when I was at the lowest point of my life many years ago, and I found myself years later making the same choice from a very low point in my life. The difference between JJ and Ben was that this time I invited God and would not move if I felt God was not moving with me. I literally asked my brother and his wife (my other prayer warriors) to pray against this relationship if it was not of God.

Relationships are such an important element of our lives, and it makes perfect sense that this is the battlefield of the enemy in our lives. Certainly, it was in mine. You could do so well in your career, but if your relationships are not healthy, they will affect all areas of your life. My relationship with Ben lasted for only four months, but was deeper than my entire marriage. I am a long-term relationship kind of girl, so the length of this one deeply troubled me. However, it had such a significant role to play in my life. In these four months, I caught a glimpse of how love plays out in a relationship. How having an innate understanding of each other is so important for a healthy foundation. However, Ben and I were not joined at the roots. He was agnostic and I was Christian, and I believe this was and would have been the eventual demise of our relationship sooner or later. What this relationship did for me was to force me to cut out friends I believed were for me, but in fact were not.

Let's go back a bit. Ben was good friends with the friend I moved in with in Cape Town, and I knew this. Over the years, my friend would talk about Ben and I would ask if she was interested in Ben in that way. She said no every time. When Ben made moves on me, I went back to my friend and revisited this conversation. She again assured me nothing was going on between her and Ben, and she did not like him like that. I proceeded with my 'relationship' with Ben. However, certain things just did not sit well with my spirit. Firstly, Ben and my friend bought each other very personal and well-thought-out gifts for their birthdays. My friend's birthday is in March, the same month I moved in with her. She booked out an entire house for her thirtieth birthday and Ben was invited. I later discovered Ben contributed half of the payment of the house. This immediately shook my spirit. I did not even think to contribute anything towards the house, and I am her friend too. So, for Ben to volunteer half of the payment made no sense to me. There were other friends invited to the house, and none of them paid.

My friend and I have been friends for years, and I look at her Instagram statuses often enough. She never posted about Ben in all the years I had known her. During the four months of my relationship with Ben, she would post old pictures of her hanging out with Ben with captions such as, "I miss the clan." I was not in any of those pictures. Ben invited me to join him for a night of jazz. I agreed, and thought it would be just the two of us. When I got to Ben's place, I found out he had invited a couple who lived in the same apartment as the friend I was living with. I did not mind this one bit. We got to the jazz and Ben asked me if he should invite my friend, given her neighbours are here and the four of them usually go to jazz. I found this strange. I mean, I thought it would be just the two of us to begin with, and he took the liberty of inviting other people. So, why was I now being asked about my friend? I refused to read much into this, but again, the nagging feeling of something being off rose up in me. This time I was adamant about not ignoring any red flags or signs. Part of my prophecy was how integral my life partner would be in my life. This was something I had always been aware of from a very young age. See, the area of your greatest destiny is the area you battle with the most. Pay extra attention to the area you face the most challenges in. In there your purpose and destiny lie.

Ben never invited my friend and I never felt the need to discuss this with her or Ben again, as I felt it was not really my concern. They just needed to manage their relationship and get a hold of their feelings, as far as I was concerned. The nagging feeling I had during the jazz and after seeing the Instagram posts was to become a recurring feeling for the duration of the four months I dated Ben. I felt it again one evening after we all congregated for an F1 game. After the game, I was waiting for Ben in his car when Ben and my friend walked out together and started hugging and holding hands. That feeling returned instantaneously. I never discussed this feeling with Ben. Firstly, he never acknowledged anything with my friend. Secondly, society truly trains us to dismiss our intuition. The world is quick to label you as insecure, jealous and all sorts of names for simply acting and inquiring based on a feeling you cannot shake. At this point I knew I had to seek out my life's arsenal and pray. For the first time in my life, I started to pray people out of my life. I invited all my prayer warriors and they stood with me in prayer. I realised a lot was at stake here if I was misreading my intuition and indeed acting out of jealousy or insecurities. This was highly possible, given everything I was going through and had gone through. I loved my friend, and I knew our friendship would be the one I would really lose in this. While I liked Ben a lot, and he will forever be dear to me for playing a part in God's revelation of what a loving relationship can be like, losing him was not the greatest loss.

Soon after praying Ben out of my life, he broke up with me. I was still living with my friend, which meant I was going to see Ben again. A week after our breakup we were all invited to a movie night at one of our friend's house. Ben was the only guy attending the movie night. The night started off great, with Ben ignoring me for the most part. I did not mind this at all. I remember talking to him briefly and saying see we can be friends after all and hang out. Ben replied that we could not. He could not fully express himself in my presence. I had no idea what this meant. But I just needed to stick around a little longer, and Ben would show me exactly what he meant. So, stick around I did. Later in the night my friend made her way onto Ben's lap. The feeling returned, but this time confirming, not questioning. Things could not get any worse. We all slept after the movie, myself sleeping on the coach. I woke up from the couch in the living room where I had taken a nap and saw Ben sneaking into the host's bedroom. He undressed and got into her bed. Minutes later, the host screamed and woke up the whole house.

I went to the room where my friend, who had sat on Ben's lap was sleeping and woke her up. Avoiding the drama I knew was about to go down, I begged her to get her car keys so we could drive back to her house. It was around three a.m. and the lockdown restrictions on travelling were still applicable. She got up and slowly looked for her keys. Not fast enough, as the host caught up with us in the kitchen, after screaming and chasing Ben out of her bed. She looked at me and asked why I did not stop Ben. I felt myself about to lose it with someone if I didn't leave. I looked at the host and reminded her how she had been flirting with Ben the whole night, and how, according to Ben, she had invited him to her bed. At this point the details were not really of concern to me. Ben was a free citizen acting out his rights and fully expressing himself. I just wanted to get out of there and not have to deal with any of it.

We drove home and went straight to bed. The next morning, I was the only one with the full details of the previous night, as everyone else claimed they were too drunk to remember. I remember thinking and feeling like I was going around in circles in my life. The same morning, I booked my flight home to my mother's house in the Eastern Cape. I knew something had to give. My friend's neighbours called me to check-in, as they heard what had transpired. I told them that I was deeply disappointed at my friend more than Ben. Ben and I had broken up, and I did not care how he chose to proceed with his life. What hurt me was my friend's behaviour throughout my brief but deep relationship with Ben, from the Instagram statuses to her siting on my ex-boyfriend's lap a week after we broke up. I had hung out with her and Ben before he and I dated, including at her birthday party at the house she rented and she never sat on Ben or acted inappropriately around him.

There was no place I wanted to be more than home. Every relationship, be it romantic or friendly, I entered between 2019 and 2021 had ended. Only the solid ones remained. Everything that could be shaken was shaken. Everything that could be taken was taken. Everything that could be lost, I lost, and everything I could gain, I gained. The biggest gains were in my career and finances. While staying with my friend in Cape Town I got the opportunity to lead a project for the Johannesburg Stock Exchange on Gender. This was my first real legacy project as an independent consultant and lead economist. I directed and conceptualised the project. I could not comprehend how I could be doing so well in one area of my life, and failing dismally, or at least feeling like it, on the other. I was experiencing first-hand the dualities of life. I learned that success can be accompanied by a mess in some area of your life.

I always imagined a linear trajectory of life, with only one direction; straight upwards. Getting my first job while still in university and marrying JJ, I believed I had begun the journey upwards on a straight line. If someone told me my career would take a squiggly turn and my romantic life would become a battlefield, I would have never believed them. But I am learning to embrace ambiguity and uncertainty. I am learning to accept being comfortable and uncomfortable at the same time. Had it not been for my faith I would have been ill-equipped for everything I faced in my life. I cannot even begin to imagine how I would have handled everything.

A Storm within a Storm

I arrived home in the Eastern Cape at the end of July in 2021. The JSE project was almost completed. I was so exhausted, and had this lingering feeling of not being anchored. This feeling began in 2019 after my divorce. It was a fleeting feeling I strongly felt some days and did not feel on most days. Being home, I felt it strongly. I remembered a holiday I had booked with a friend in Mossel Bay in 2020, but did not take due to lockdown regulations. I thought to myself that if I got some air after wrapping up the JSE project and just went and read my Bible quietly by the beach in Mossel Bay, my spirit would be at peace once more. I was longing for the peace that surpasses all understanding, which I had not felt on a daily basis in years.

I reached out to a friend of mine who had been going through the most as well, and we agreed to go to Mossel Bay at the end of August. We booked our flights and agreed to meet at the Cape Town airport and drive down to Mossel Bay. The day before my flight departed for Cape Town, my friend reached out and showed me the weather forecast. Rain was predicted for the whole week. She asked if we should cancel. I said we should proceed. In my mind, rain would not affect much as all I wanted was solitude and to read my Bible. I told my mother about the rain forecast and she too suggested we postpone. I asked her how long it should be for. Who was to say it would not rain on the said future date? I proceeded to the airport and got on my flight. My friend and I met in Cape Town and drove town to Mossel Bay.

There was a sombre atmosphere throughout the trip, at least for me. My feeling of being unanchored came back. I remember two distinct cases we almost got into a car accident on our way to Mossel Bay. The first was inside the tunnel exiting Cape Town, and the second time was around Stellenbosch. Despite all this and my feeling, we arrived in Mossel Bay and enjoyed our holiday. The feeling came back just before I went ziplining. Again, I dismissed it, and this time I thought it was my fear of heights. Throughout the trip I do not remember reading my Bible, not even once. I took it out every morning, but never got around to opening it.

The morning of our drive back to Cape Town, the feeling of being unanchored came back strongly. It was my friend's turn to drive. I remember debating with myself if I should not perhaps drive. I decided to let her get started and I would take over later in the journey, a decision I would later thank myself for. It was not long since we had commenced our journey. We were forty-five minutes into a five-hour journey when a bakkie came from behind us trying to overtake into oncoming traffic. Halfway through his manoeuvre he realised he was not going to make it, as there was a truck on the other side overtaking another truck. He decided to hit us and took us off the road. I remember seeing the two trucks, one carrying logs, ahead of us and feeling the bump on the side of our car. I looked at my friend's helpless and frightened face asking what had happened. I knew exactly what was happening. I did not answer her, but started praying and grabbed my Bible.

You see, God and I had been on a trial run of this in 2019. In April of 2019, after dropping JJ at the airport, I got into a horrible car accident which I escaped without a scratch. My car got written off. JJ had never asked me to drive him to the airport because he knew how much I dreaded driving, especially on the freeway. He knew our policy was take the train unless the flight was way before the first train. He absolutely could have taken the train that day, but he wanted to be dropped off. I dropped him at the airport and headed home. On my way home again, two trucks were overtaking each other on the slower lanes. I was on the fast lane and one of the rubber coverings from the truck's tires came loose and fell on my lane. I was coming fast, and I had a split second to make a decision. I knew if I immediately slowed down someone was going to hit me from behind. What I did not know was what would happen if I tried to drive over the rubber. One thing I knew was that my car was not solid enough, and I was not going to test it by attempting to go over a rubber cover from an eighteen-wheeler.

I slowed my car as best I could, put on my hazards, took my feet off the pedals and started praying. I was right. While implementing my manoeuvres, I felt a bang at the back of my car. I spun around on the freeway and hit the concrete slab on the road before hitting another car and facing oncoming traffic. To my surprise, I was conscious and alive. Immobilised by shock, I sat in my car without a clue what to do. I could see the danger I was in and realised the possibility of someone hitting me again. This happened at dawn around four a.m. while it was still dark. Thank God a motorbike rider who had a reflective jacket on stopped. He came on the road, tried to control the traffic, and took me out of the car. The car-towing guys arrived on the scene. It took about an hour for my brain to function again. The police and ambulance had not yet arrived. Recognising I was fine, I asked the towing guys to drive me home. They did. I got home and made a cup of tea. I sat and calmly drunk my tea. I went to bed and took a nap.

I had not fully comprehended what I had just gone through. During my nap my back started hurting. JJ was back in the house. He said he tried to call me and when I did not pick up, he knew something had happened and he did not get on the plane. He rushed me to the hospital, and they performed tests and scans and found nothing.

The second time around, my friend and I were not going to escape that easily. After grabbing my Bible and praying I lost consciousness. According to eyewitnesses we got knocked off the road, hit a storm water drain first, and flew several times in the air before our car landed on the side of the road. They said it was like watching a scene from a movie. The eyewitness quoted by the newspaper article that reported the car accident did not expect to see us alive. Several car crashes had been reported on that stretch of road since January of that year, and not a single survivor was reported.

I was seriously injured, slipping in and out of consciousness. My friend had to be pulled out using the jaws of life which completely crushed her legs. I remember waking up for a split second when the paramedics arrived. I was pulled out through the window, and I lost consciousness again. Next time I woke up I was in the first hospital, a government hospital, and I was fighting for my life. My friend's child was in the hospital.

I managed to say, "Hello," before losing consciousness again.

I later woke up at the second hospital, a private hospital. This time I was on my way to the operating room. I was in a terrible state. I felt it. My mother received that call no parent ever wants to get. The doctors were giving me a fifty-fifty chance of surviving this, and urged my mother to get to George immediately. Ever the prayer warrior, my mom says she firstly could not comprehend anything that was being said to her. In her mind, her daughter was on her way to Cape Town. We had spoken over the phone just before we left Mossel Bay for Cape Town. She says it hit her when the second call from my brother came.

My mother is the epitome of grace and poise. I have never seen my mother angry in thirty-two years. She exudes dignity. After speaking to my brother, she got on her knees and prayed. After praying, she cleaned her house and called my aunt, another prayer warrior. During trauma you lose consciousness of time. I am not sure how long it took my mother to complete her rituals before making it to George. All I know is that for me, waiting for her arrival felt like eternity. My brother was the first to arrive. While I appreciated seeing my brother, it was not the face I wanted to see. I wanted my mommy. I was crying for my mother.

After two days of operations and enduring twenty-four-hours anaesthesia, I was still in very critical condition. I had all the tubes you can imagine running through my nose, mouth, lungs and everywhere. I had only ever seen so many wires and tubes on a person in movies. When I started gaining consciousness and woke up in ICU, I can honestly admit now that I lost my sanity for a while. Nothing was medically wrong with my brain, but the trauma I felt caused me to believe I had gone bonkers for two seconds. I had dreams and hallucinations and saw things that did not happen. I vividly remember driving in a car around the hospital with my brother, who later confirmed this did not happen. I believed one nurse in particular, sister Mary, was poisoning me. I also remember one nurse telling me I was not going to make it out alive. While I may not be sure if these happened in my head or really happened, I find it strange that the names of the nurses where true. I insisted not to see these two nurses in particular. There was one nurse who calmed my soul and prayed with me every time she was on duty.

I spent a total of two months in hospital. I was incubated for several days and was bedridden for six weeks. I had to learn how to control my breathing to avoid being reintubated. Now, learning to breathe in a controlled manner is not a task for the faint-hearted, especially when you are going through so many emotions at once. You experience first-hand how certain emotions affect your organs. The minute I became angry, one of the screens would beep, and I would struggle to breathe. When anxiety kicked in, another monitor would beep and another organ was immediately impacted. I remember praying constantly and asking how it was that I found myself in this situation, and yet it seemed I was expected to feel nothing. Every time an emotion hit, something would beep on my screen, causing me more panic and frustration.

God spoke to me so clearly through the song "Be Still

and Know that I am your God." I had to learn to still my emotions and completely trust that God was there for me. I sang this song so many times it became the theme song for the critical six weeks of my hospitalization. I relinquished every emotion and form of control to God. I thought to myself that if God wanted me dead, then I would be dead already. There was no way He would bring me this far just to leave me. The minute I realised and accepted this thought, I had such peace. I stopped fighting the nurses. At this point, you are probably wondering how a bedridden and intubated person is fighting nurses. You'd best believe I was, to the point that they had to chain my hands to the sides of the bed. I do not recall what my fighting style was initially, but according to the nurses I was removing all the tubes and throwing things at them. Remember, I was slipping in and out of consciousness, and being in a state of trauma meant for me time had come to a standstill. So, let's rely on the nurses' account here. But in retrospect, and knowing myself, I do not believe I was removing the tubes out of anger. Yes, I was angry, I have no doubt about that. Who wouldn't be? But I genuinely believe I thought I was fine, and I was probably trying to get to Cape Town as that was the last memory of where I was meant to be. My brain had not completely made sense of what was happening and where I was versus where I was going before the accident.

I know this, as there were some mornings I would wake up thinking I was in my hotel and wake up to my reality and start panicking and crying. I had tubes down my throat and my hands were tied up so I couldn't even ask anyone anything. This completely threw me off. The minute I came to my senses and realised exactly where I was, I started attempting to get rid of my hand ties. I just wanted to express myself somehow. I figured by writing something I could at least tell these nurses that I wouldn't remove the tubes again and we could communicate through written notes. My brother would come in and I would try to communicate this to him using tied up hands and my eyes. I never had such great value and respect for the ability to be able to communicate non-verbally with someone and being in sync with someone. In my head, I was telling him to untie my hands through my eyes and tapping on the side on the bed. It took several visits for him to finally understand me. When he eventually got my message, he told me it was for my own safety, and he did not remove them or even ask the nurses. Once again, through my eyes and tapping, I tried to tell him I was over that stage of alleged self-harm, and all I wanted was to communicate now.

My mother still had not arrived at this stage, and I knew she would be the only person to understand me and remove these hand ties. Feeling defeated, I realised nothing was going to come from my brother or the nurses. I did not even bother to ask the nurses, because I knew that for them having one less patient with access to the bell to call them was a major win. I started fiddling with the bandages used to tie my hands until they came loose. But I waited for my brother to return before using my hands, fearing that if the nurses saw me, they would tie me up again. My brother came every day, sometimes twice a day. When he came, I asked him to bring me a pen and paper using my now free hands.

He looked for them and brought them. One of the nurses asked if he untied me. He said that he found me loose, and thought it was them. I sensed the nurse's frustration because no way was I going to allow them to tie me up this time. I was now fully conscious and aware that I was in hospital and not in my hotel or heading for Cape Town. I wrote my brother quite a lengthy and firm letter with very strict instructions not to be tied again. I asked him to go buy me my own notebook and pen and put them next to me. I also inquired what was taking my mother so long. Before my mother even told me what delayed her upon her eventual arrival, I imagined her cleaning the house, panicking, and trying to pack the best clothes before leaving. All the things many would see as unnecessary, but only her and I would have the audacity to do in an emergency.

I wrote to my brother on the note pad to please insist that my mother kindly drop everything and jump on the first flight to George. I specifically instructed my brother to book the flight himself, knowing that if left to my mother she would find a reason to delay even further. And she did. I instructed my brother, who had booked himself at a hotel next door, to leave immediately and see to this. He left. I am not sure how the communication went between the two of them. All I knew was that I was dying to see my mother. She was the only person I wanted by my side. It was not my first time in hospital, and every time I had been there with my mother. The first time I was in grade one when I woke up blind. I was hospitalized for three weeks. My mother never left my side. The second time I was in grade five and came down with TB and pneumonia. I was hospitalized for a month plus. Again, we made this journey together with my mom.

My mother managed to convince my brother that

driving to George would be a good idea, instead of flying. She eventually got to the hospital with my aunt. I asked her what took her so long. She told me everything I already knew. How it took a while for all of it to sink in. And when it did, how she oscillated between praying and cleaning and packing and all sorts of things. She said it was when she spoke to my uncle that she realised the urgency of her arrival. My uncle told her that her child would not be well unless she went there to be with her. She says when she heard this, she dropped everything and felt the urgency to get to the hospital.

It is one thing to be physically okay. It is something else to not lose hope. While waiting for my mother to arrive. I realised the machines were doing a great job in keeping me alive, but life or death resided in my spirit. I knew if I lost the battle inside and lost hope then my body would surely follow. I also knew if I held on inside and did not lose faith my organs would follow, and it would be a matter of time before I was off these machines. I had to find the will to live. My mother had always had the ability to speak life to me when I had felt like letting go during my previous hospitalisations. This time I was missing my trooper. I was so close to giving up. Had she taken any longer, she probably would have made it in time to pick up the body of her daughter.

Life immediately returned to my spirit when I saw my mother and aunt walk into the room. My fighting spirit came back. Within days doctors were seeing improvements. My lungs recovered, and the tubes and wires sustaining them were removed. My breathing became more regular. Within days, the doctor looking after me said they could try to reduce the number of tubes supporting my breathing. I looked at him and saw that he feared making this call again. See, he had made this call about a week earlier, before my mother had arrived, with such confidence, and I struggled to breathe and slipped back into unconsciousness and had to be reintubated. I tried to reassure him that this time would be fine, and that I had my pillar of strength. Cautious not to make the same mistake again, he said they would give it a day or two, but that I had to promise him to handle my breathing and emotions.

Tube by tube they started falling. My swelling came down within a day of seeing my mother. I went from being bathed on the bed by no less than four nurses at a time to needing one nurse. The recovery and healing continued until my release date. My mother never left until I was discharged, and we came home together.

Some of my friends who came to visit asked me what my big 'Aha' moment was. I did not have an 'Aha' moment. Maybe it is still to come. For me, it was still God's voice I heard. I saw His character in a way I had never seen or understood it before. He was adamant on showing me His love. All I could read was my Bible. My therapist gave me so many books, but not even one captured my interest. I read my Bible like never before. I started with the book of Job, a story I knew but could never bring myself to read. The funny thing was that a year before during Connect (a church meeting), we talked about the book of Job, and I shared how I found it depressing and always skipped it. I felt a nudge after Connect to read the book of Job, but I never did until my time in hospital. I saw how much God loved Job and trusted that he would never run away from

Him even in the hardest of times. Very few people stick during hard times. Even in the Christian family, I have met so many people who turn away from God when they hit hard times. They question God's goodness and love. I mean, as a student of philosophy I am well aware that the question those who do not believe in God ask is, "If God is good, why does He allow bad things to happen?"

I remember saying to one of my friends during a visit that God must be punishing me. This was absolutely not true. After I deliberately immersed myself in His word with the sole purpose of understanding His character, my perspective and understanding of everything that had happened to me completely changed. Firstly, I realized God was not punishing me. I realised that all of this was happening primarily because of the purpose God has for my life. I realised that I must have something that is threatening to the devil for him to have had a target on my life since birth. And I realised that God has been with me. He stopped every weapon formed from prospering. I looked at the car and I looked at myself and I could not believe my eyes. Everyone who saw the car was shocked to see my physical condition. That's when I realised God fought for me. I played out all the scenarios and mine was absolutely not the worst-case scenario. I know some might say this is negative positivity, but it isn't. It is the truth. However, it is a truth that one can only see in time. If someone told me this in the moment, I would not have seen nor appreciated it. But with time, it's a perspective that has helped me in moving on.

God having a purpose for my life means I have a mission to accomplish on this Earth. It may be as simple as my testimony to someone who will read this book and feel God's glory in their life. Purpose does not have to be grandiose or on a big scale. It can be as simple as ministering to just the people in your immediate environment. I knew God was definitely working through me in the lives of those around me by the sheer spectacle of my accident, and even some of the things that happened to me prior my accident. I had been sick before, and no one knew except my nuclear family. I was in a car accident before, but no one knew except JJ and my immediate family. I do not share my private life beyond those affected by it. Even the closest of my friends will tell you how private I am about my life. This time around, God was forcing me to open up and was showing off, not for my sake, but for His glory.

I have always been praying for God to reveal my purpose. I realised that my purpose and the point of my existence on this Earth is for God to do His work through my life. Much like Job; God was not punishing Job, Job was blameless. But God chose someone He knew would not quit Him to minister to Job's friends through Job. I am not sure exactly who God is targeting through my story, but I know everyone who witnessed me between 2019 and now in-person and everyone who will read this book and hear my story is definitely a target audience. For someone who struggles with vulnerability, God absolutely had to force me to be vulnerable.

Secondly, I was not seeking 'Aha' moments or even understanding during all of this. See, in my walk of faith I had become comfortable long ago with not knowing why things happen. Faith is the trust and hope in things unseen.

This even helped me make some of the biggest career decisions in my life, like quitting a permanent job in investment banking with so many possibilities and venturing into a career I felt a strong calling to: politics with no seen possibilities or no clear trajectory.

I needed to hear His voice saying, "I am not punishing you. I am with you." And I heard Him loudly and clearly.

I re-examined my injuries, and I saw Him in all of them. He took just enough from me to always rely on him and know he is with me. Not to break and crush my soul, but to give me a new life that is completely dependent and reliant upon Him.

Surviving the Storm

This is the most important chapter of the book. It's primarily the reason I decided to write it in the first place. I wanted to help anyone going through difficult times, whatever they are, to not lose hope. To never see the things that happen to them as working against them, but for them. I believe the minute you alter your perspective into seeing how things are working for you and not against you, you begin the most powerful journey of your life. You tap into reservoirs you did not even know you had. You unleash a powerful you that you yourself have not met. You get introduced to the person you know always existed in your heart, but never had the opportunity to encounter.

Your storm, place of dryness, your wilderness, whatever you call it, is a very important place and time in your life. This is where you do most of your growing as a person. In China, they have a saying that you are not a businessman until your business has failed at least twice. There is a lot of truth in this. You honestly learn a lot in spaces and places where you are not compared to places where you are. Let me clarify too that your place of dryness, wilderness or storm is not a place of failure at all. It's the place where you face your greatest challenges in life. You can attribute how you get here to failure if you will, but I argue how you get to this place is rather a secondary question. Your primary concern should be what lessons you need to learn to not only ensure you make it to the end of the storm, but to also ensure you never go through the same kind of storm again. For me, failure would be giving in and giving up during the storm. I honestly believe in life, whether it is in starting your business, your workout regime, or your personal life, you only lose if you give up.

There are lessons and revelations that only come through adversity. This alone should encourage you not to run away from adversity or pray it away, but to take it head-on and await the joy that only comes at the end. Is this easier said than done? Absolutely. I wanted to slap everyone that uttered or alluded to this during my storms, especially in the beginning. If you are at the beginning of your storm, I sympathise with you wanting to put this book down, but I commend you for making it this far. In the beginning stages of my storm I had everything dry up. No jobs were coming my way. I was back in my mother's house nursing broken body parts which limited my mobility. All of which forced me to be still and present in the storm. It is in that place of stillness and being fully present that I began to see the lessons and revelations of my storm.

I heard God's voice and plan for my life so clearly. You see, whether you believe in God or not, your life is always guiding you. The question is: are you willing to listen? Listening means setting time aside for solitude. Listening means not going against the waves of what is happening in your life, but actually being still and move in the direction of the waves. Ask any swimmer, and they will tell you how tiring and dangerous it is to try and swim against the current. You can actually lose your life. Being silent means moving away from all forms of distraction, willingly or forcefully. We tend to think of distractions as things and people that are bad for us. But no, your biggest distractions come in the form of things you enjoy the most and 'good' people.

It is in my place of 'wilderness' that I for the first time became obedient to God. I came to the point in my life where I did not want anything that I felt would move me away from my faith and the work God was doing inside of me. I wanted to know God for myself and not through what I have been taught about Him. I believe the biggest danger and obstacle those seeking God's face is delegating this expedition to others, whether it is your family, your preacher, or even the friends in your life who seem to have it all together in their walk of faith. The most important relationship God cares about is the intimate one He has with all of us individually, not through any medium.

It is in my place of wilderness where I started not only to dream again but to dream at an even greater scale than before. I surrendered all areas of my life, including my relationships, to God. Not only did God direct me towards the areas and people I needed to focus on, He also showed me my 'why.' I found the greatest motivation to not give up, and the strength to continue going after my dreams in my place of wilderness. I relied so much on my family during this time, from my daily walks with my brother and uncle to my niece helping me put on my shoes, that I remembered why I had a burning fire in my heart to be great. I am never moved by money or riches. For me, modelling to my family what is possible beyond their imagination has always motivated me. I realised how important family is to me. Family speaks to a very important aspect of God. All God has done and will do is generational. We see it in the book of Ruth, Abraham, and many other examples in the Bible.

Any time before 2018, if someone had met me and told me all that was to come and that I would not only survive but I would come out stronger than before with a new zeal for life, I would have never believed them. I did not just get to this point though. Ask my friends who visited me in hospital and at home. It was like meeting a new person every time. My perspective and attitude shifted with time, the biggest gift we are all equally endowed with.

I have met very few people in life who have not come across a storm or two, or even more, in their lives. Storms are about as sure as sunshine in this journey of life. Yes, they are all different, and we all have different natural and acquired endowments. We either survive them or wither away with them. An equally true and guaranteed fact of a storm is that it must end. Its end is assured. However, knowing this, believing it, conceiving of it, and seeing this in the middle of the storm are each a different story. There are many factors that play a huge role in one's ability to know, believe, conceive, and see the end of the storm in the middle of the storm.

Surround yourself with people who speak life to you.

I went from feeling like I was being punished and deserved everything that was happening to me to believing that everything I had gone through, whether earned or not, was working for my good. I actually decided to completely abandon all thoughts of the 'worthiness' of my misfortunes, and focused on the person I wanted to be at the end of it all. I did not just get to this realisation. After immersing myself in the book of Job during my hospitalisation, I still faced a challenge. See, in the book it clearly says Job was blameless. Come now, I absolutely did not live a blameless life. I had to wrestle with this. I started by talking to my friends about it and, much like Job's friends, they agreed I was not blameless. Some, one, tacitly said I deserved everything that was happening. My own sister explicitly told me how evil I was and how I deserved everything that was happening to me. I cannot over-emphasise the importance of the people around you during your hardest times and the words spoken by those around you. I admit, lying in hospital it is hard to decide who has access to you or not. George is not an easy place to get to so when friends and family came, it would seem very rude to ask them leave. There are two people in particular where my heart sunk upon their visitation.

While you may not have complete control on who has access to you in your most vulnerable time, please resist the urge to believe everything thrown at you. I needed to remind myself that my sister and I never grew up together. We do not have any personal relationship except that she is my sister. She doesn't know anything about my life, and she is speaking from a place of observation, not a place of knowledge. So, why would I believe someone I have no relationship with about who I am, when I know myself and must deal with myself every day? It took time for me to flip this. The words hurt and pierced me at the time because I was in an emotionally vulnerable position. Once I got to this realisation, I even reached out to her in an effort to show her that I harbour no resentment or bad feelings towards her.

My brother called me during the summer holidays, two months after being discharged and having this encounter with my sister. He was speaking about something completely different, but relevant. He said he and his wife were overcome by a spirit to pray over words that will be spoken to me during this difficult time. I think back and I thank God for all the people He has placed in my life. Make no mistake: whatever situation you face, those who know about it will have an opinion on it. Some will have the wisdom to know when and what to say to you. Others will not, and these are the dangerous people during a storm.

While I had people like my brother and other supportive friends who called and prayed with me, I needed more positive reinforcements on the nature of God. I needed people who just have the gift of speaking life into people. A friend of mine, one of the positive reinforcements, gave me a book by Bishop TD Jakes, *Crushing*. This book, together with his sermons I found online, helped me a great deal in understanding pain for purpose.

I immediately disassociated from certain people. Others gladly walked out of their own accord. I only kept my lines of communication open to those people that were speaking life to me. I realised you are better off with one person during your storm who speaks life into you than twenty people who leave a mark of uncertainty in your spirit.

Never forget your history with God

While still battling the thoughts that plagued me of not being blameless like Job, I had to remind myself of the history I had with God. I took out my journal and started writing all the good things God had done for me, going back as far as kindergarten. See, when the enemy and your mind want to play tricks with you and convince you that you are a bad person, make no mistake, they will go as far back as the time in kindergarten you lied about not eating in class to your teacher. I wrote down every good thing God had ever done for me. To my surprise, the list was actually long. This exercise breathed in new life in my heart. I found myself asking, if God is all knowing and was punishing me, why would He leave a trail of His goodness for me to remember? Surely if He was punishing me and wanted me to perish, He would have made sure I had nothing good to draw from my reservoirs. I imagined myself and what I would do if I was punishing someone. Well, you make sure they have absolutely no recourse. I realised I was seeing and understanding God and my troubles in the eyes of the natural, and not through God's eyes.

Feeling uplifted, I went through all my pictures, emails, and any record I could find looking for all the amazing things God had done for me. I went into my Instagram page and took down all my pictures, and started putting up all the pictures of all the places God had taken me to. It was also through this exercise that I felt a nudge to reach out to people God had exposed in my life under supernatural circumstances who had a deep impact in my life.

Looking at my injuries, I realised how I had gotten TB and pneumonia before, while I had a fully functioning spleen. And realised that I had nothing to fear with the removal of my spleen after the accident. I studied biology in high school, and never learned about a spleen until the day my doctor was explaining it to me and why they had to remove it. I asked myself why I would fear an organ I did not even know I had prior the accident. If God was for me, who and what could be against me?

I felt God telling me, "I am the author and finisher of your story. Nothing happens to you without my permission.

You not having a spleen means nothing to me." I remembered how He opened my eyes when no doctor knew what had shut them in the first place.

My uncle shared Psalm 91 with me. I woke up every day for months, and I still do today, and recite this scripture and proclaim it over my life. Verses 3, 6, 7 and 10 spoke life to me and helped me overcome my fear of not having a spleen in the midst of a pandemic. I tried to find stories online of people without a spleen. Well, we are a rare bunch, especially in South Africa. Anyhow, what this journey of seeking people's stories did for me was to show me the importance of storytelling. It encouraged me to find ways to share my story.

You have a history with God. Whether you know it or not, He has been fighting for you, and He continues to fight for you. If you have never seen Him come out and show off in your life, I urge you to walk the walk of faith and believe those of us who have personally had many encounters with Him.

Allow Time to become your Friend

I believe we step into a new dimension when we start praying for God to close doors and remove people and things from our lives that are not for our good. Ever the workaholic, I was eager to go back to my 'normal' life. While in hospital I took a job interview. I can now look back and thank God for all my injuries. He broke me in all the right places that would slow me down and force me to not go anywhere before He was done pressing me. I remember having an interview in my mother's house for a job in

Johannesburg. My back just would not give. Although the doctors had cleared me to go back to work with certain conditions but my back was just not budging. He shut all opportunities that would not serve His purpose in my life. While in hospital, I began praying like this. I knew I did not come this far with God so He could leave me. I also realised that everything was serving His purpose, and I did not want anything or anyone in my life that would move me away from that.

I did not get the job I interviewed for while in hospital, and He would go on to close many such opportunities. I went back to my mother's house. A colleague of mine reached out and in our conversation, she told me not to be eager to go back to anything, but to allow myself all the time in the world. Noticing the silence and closing of opportunities, I welcomed this. I started minimising my social media presence until I reached the point that going online would not entice me in any form or shape. I muted certain statuses that were not serving my decision to behold my situation in my mother's house. I spoke to my mother and she confirmed a timeline that was in my heart, to stay for a year with her. This was a hard pill to swallow. I welcomed it and completely embraced it. I stopped even searching for opportunities that required me to leave before a year was up.

Settling into the idea of time being my healer and possibly the best arsenal was not an easy task. Not in a world where you are constantly bombarded by people's success and seemingly moving lives, while yours feels like it has taken a hard knock. But I tell you, sometimes the greatest growth happens in your place of 'stagnation.' It's here I learned to celebrate the victories of my friends. To me, they become a living example of what I had to hope for and hold onto. I believed there is no way God has favourites, but in His word He tells us about seasons. I embraced the season I was in, and it was a season of crushing, pruning, and beholding. Understanding life as a series of seasons is so important. It sheds jealousy, inadequacy, doubt, and all sorts of other feelings that can overwhelm you and make you feel like you have done nothing with your life. In truth, you probably have done a lot, at the very least enough to take you to the next level of your life.

God will provide even in the place of 'dryness' in your life. He is a good God and a father who wants nothing but to shower you with His reckless love. Allow Him to. I found jobs to do remotely that I did not even apply for. I remember listening to a sermon by Stephanie Ike. She was talking about what God did in her life during a time she found herself in the 'wilderness'. She mentioned how opportunities will find you that are from God, because He is not an author of confusion. He will make sure you know it is Him sending you manna.

Once I accepted things would take time, and decided to allow myself time and not be rushed into anything by external or internal forces, God revealed so much to me. I absolutely would not have written this book otherwise. I always had the sense that I should write a book about my story, but I always wanted to see the end first before I wrote it. I wanted to sort of be standing on the top of the hill and shout before writing. But in this time of 'beholding,' I realised that is not where the power of my story is. It is so easy to shout and thank God when standing on the top of the hill, but it takes courage and faith to thank Him in the midst of your difficulty. It means you understand who He is. He will never fail you. But it also means you are in a very powerful place spiritually and in your life, where you are okay with however your story ends. You do not need grand gestures that are visible to the world for you to thank God and love Him.

God has performed His biggest miracles for me, and I am certain for you too. Anything else He will add is a bonus and a true testament to who He is. The fact that I can breathe again, walk again and am in a healthy state is enough. I understand and can appreciate that this fact will only ever be appreciated by those who have almost lost their lives or are in hospital or have their health and lives challenged somehow. I have read so many books that write about how health is wealth. I never fully appreciated this until I almost lost mine. You see, whatever gifts and talents you have, they mean nothing without a body to carry you around and help you implement them. Even all your financial riches become absolutely worthless without a body to enjoy them with. Therefore make no mistake, your body is a temple that gives your soul permission on this earth.

Allow God to lead and guide you

"My sheep listen to my voice; I know them, and they follow me. I give them eternal life, and they will never perish. No one can snatch them away from me, for my father has given them to me, and He is more powerful than anyone else." John 10: 27-29.

I always knew I was a strong-willed person, and for me submission does not come easy. I thank God for His relentless love for me. For pursuing me even when I pursued everything else but Him. Whether you choose to listen or not, God is always speaking to you. He speaks through the voices in your soul about the things you ought to do but never seem to get around to. But they never leave you. I discovered that you can either choose to be obedient and listen to these voices, or go about your life with the idea that you'll get around to them eventually. I strongly urge you to listen to the former.

God is a God of the impossible, and will find creative ways to get your attention. When I stopped going against the tides in my life, I finally heard the voice of God and fully submitted to His plans. The biggest trick of the enemy is tricking you into believing that God only speaks to certain people. This is absolutely not true. God speaks to us every day, and we have direct access to Him. God does not speak to you with a loud voice from heaven, though He could. It's that silent voice that urges you to take a different route today. He speaks through the decisions you make, the decisions of others, sometimes your favourite preacher, and most importantly through His word. He speaks through the ideas in your heart that never leave you. Only you know and can discern when God is speaking to you.

I began to pray and fast. I moved away from all things distracting my attention away from God while still in my mother's house. It is remarkable the things I started to experience. God started addressing and healing the trauma of my accident and everything that had happened to me. Whether I deserved them or not made no difference, but I heard Him say it was not in vain. I read the story of Paul in the Bible and understood how pain and suffering are the foundations of a remarkable character.

In 2 Corinthians 4:8-9, Paul writes, "We are afflicted in every way, but never crushed; perplexed, but not driven to despair; persecuted, but not forsaken; struck down, but not destroyed." God revealed to me the very nature of being a Christian. Christianity has a cross as the marker of the religion, signifying the death of Jesus on the cross and His resurrection. In the Bible, it clearly states that we will go through a lot of suffering, but we will overcome every battle. I believe the refusal to accept that even you, yes you, are not exempt from challenges, pain and suffering is the beginning of a journey towards self-destruction. Acceptance of the fact that you are not immune or exempt from the vicissitudes of life marks the journey to your true healing.

The more I leaned in and sought God the more healing and peace I found. My morning routine for the last fifteen years entailed waking up at four a.m., going to gym for an hour and spending time with God for an hour. Even during my marriage, I never broke this, to the point that mornings I spent doing anything else highly disturbed me. God spoke to me through online sermons. But this time, all the sermons were speaking of the prophecy I had received in 2019. I found myself reaching out to people I had not spoken to in years who shifted the direction of my dreams and breathed life into them. The whole time, I had been eager to rush back to Johannesburg. I won't lie, I was not thinking bigger than South Africa. But the sermons would speak about how great our God is. That anything of Him is bound to be on an international and generational scale. During one of my conversations with a friend I had not spoken to in ten years, not only did I spark his fire, but he said something I believe altered the course of my thinking and dreams. He urged me to think and do something I had never done before. Before having this conversation with him, I had been online looking for possible opportunities in what seemed to have become a very dry part of my life. I saw a fellowship in D.C. at the World Bank. Coming across it, I found all the reasons to talk myself out of it.

I used my age as an excuse, despite the fact I was still within the age requirement. I thought I had invested too much time into my career to go begin again with a fellowship for a year. After speaking to my friend, I went back again and applied for the fellowship. While I did not get it, it allowed me to think bigger than South Africa. I remembered my prophecy, which alluded to me doing things at a global scale one day, and the sermons I was listening to that also spoke about an international God. There is a famous picture of a house on top of a house. The bottom house is a nice comfortable mansion representing the vision we have, while the top house is a gigantic house representing the magnitude of God's plan for our lives. I began to think and dream on a bigger level. While I did not get the fellowship, it completely altered my vision. I wanted God's plan for my life more than ever. I realised my dreams could only go as far as my imagination of all things conceivable, but God's plan was incomprehensible, and I wanted it.

God will lead you into places you never imagined yourself in. He will take you to rooms you never thought existed or you belonged in. I remembered how God had not only made provision for me to go to One Young World, but how He prepared a seat for me on the top floor of the Westin Hotel with the Global CEO of Barclays to discuss pressing challenges faced by the bank at twenty-one years of age. I remembered how Jamie Oliver had prepared and served us lunch in that meeting.

His word clearly says, "He will set before you a table to feast in the presence of your enemies." I have no doubt He will do it again. Psalm 37: 23 clearly stated; "The Lord directs the steps of the godly."

To the readers reading that are not believers: Firstly, I commend and thank you for sticking with me until this stage. As I mentioned in the beginning, this is not a book seeking to convince or convert anyone. If I managed to do this through sharing my experience, then it is a consequence I welcome and rejoice in. The purpose of the book is to encourage those going through hard times to know that fighting for your life is worth it. To know that there is indeed a call on your name, whether you have accepted it or not. Your life has purpose, and it matters. You matter. Jesus came on this Earth to die for everyone, not Christians. He is close to the broken-hearted. Just open yourself up just a little bit to the idea that there is someone bigger who knew you before you were even formed in your mother's womb, who longs to be reacquainted with you. Know that He wants to reveal himself in your life too if you invite Him. God gave us a will and He will never violate it. He will only come into your life by invitation.

Dream Again

I purposefully chose to write this this book while God is still drafting my story. He is the author and finisher of my story. The book is specifically aimed at helping those weathering storms to realise that their storms are not the end of their journey. They are a divine setup for where they are going. Trust the process, and know that everything is working for your good, even when you cannot see how your story ends. Faith is believing in the things unseen. It is so easy to write a motivational book once faith is realised, but I daresay the greatest faith comes in believing in the things yet to be seen and realised. I believe it is exactly this stage of the battle that sets apart those who lose from those who win. In my undergraduate conflict studies course, we studied guerrilla warfare. The biggest strategy of guerrilla wars is to fatigue their opposition. They will face a professional army with the mindset that you only lose if you quit. This is true for our life's battles. We only lose if we quit. I draw my strength from my faith and my community. To believers, I urge you to lean on your faith and press in like never before. To non-believers, find things that inspire you not to quit. Do not underestimate the power of your community.

Returning to my mother's house, the house I grew up in but had spent very little time in, I saw first-hand the importance of community. From my brother and uncle who selflessly gave up their time to take walks with me in my healing journey, to my neighbours who offered themselves to also walk with me, and to pray for me and my family. I realised for the first time that my life is not just about myself, but my immediate and wider community.

I faced and overcame my biggest fears in the warm arms of my community. Dr Bruce D. Perry and Oprah Winfrey wrote in their book *What Happened to You* that the best form of healing trauma is prolonged interactions in a loving community. They wrote that these interactions are far better than forty-five minutes of therapy. I absolutely agree. In hospital, my medical insurance insisted on therapy twice a week during my recovery time there. While I have no doubt these sessions were beneficial, they are not where my healing came from. Firstly, they were badly timed. The entire two months in hospital I was oscillating between the stages of shock and denial and there is no way healing can come while you have not even accepted and fully comprehended all that has happened to you.

Being home and completely surrendering to God and something bigger than myself provided me with the holistic healing I did not even know I needed. It is here I allowed myself to hope again. To dream again. To reimagine. To question all I thought I knew, and find the courage to begin again. It is here I was introduced to a Nomahlubi Jakuja I knew existed, but had never met before. It is here a realised a strength and fortitude I did not know I had. Our greatest fear is abandoning an image of our self we crafted in our minds of who we thought we were, the image celebrated by those around us. We must step into the space that allows us to meet a self we have never met before, and allow the new self to take us to places we never thought possible, at least for us.

Beginning again opens you up to access new heights your old self would not have dared to enter. The more we achieve unquestioned and unchallenged success, the more comfortable we get with the ways that got us to that success. Challenges and life's forced pitstops are remarkable in that they cause you to stop and rethink your ways, and find new ways to imagine a future you did not even know was possible. Do not despise challenges in whatever form they come in. Allow them to challenge your known knowns and reveal your unknown unknowns. For I believe the best version of yourself, and your greatest success, lie in discovering your unknown unknowns.

God is still writing my story, and I look forward to the next chapter of my life and the amazing things to come.